Pacman Frogs

Pacman frogs as pets.

Housing, costs, care, diet, grooming, training and health.

by

David Golderton

Table of Contents

Introduction

I want to thank you and congratulate you for buying the book 'Pacman frogs as pets'. This book will help you to understand everything you need to know about domesticating a Pacman frog. You will learn all the aspects related to raising the Pacman frog successfully at home. You will be able to understand the pros and cons, behavior, basic care, keeping, housing, diet and health related to the animal.

There are people who are impressed by the adorable looks of the Pacman frog. They think that this reason is enough to domesticate the animal, but domestication of a Pacman frog has its unique challenges and issues.

If you are not ready for these challenges, then you are not ready to domesticate the animal. If you have already bought or adopted a Pacman frog, even then you need to understand your pet so that you take care of him in a better way. It is important that you understand that owning any pet will have its advantages and disadvantages.

You should see whether with all its pros and cons, the animal fits well into your household. Domesticating and taming a pet is not only fun. There is a lot of hard work that goes into it. It is important that you are ready to commit before you decide to domesticate the animal. If you are a prospective buyer, then understanding these points will help you to make a wise decision.

When you bring a pet home, it becomes your responsibility to raise the pet in the best way possible. You have to provide physically, mentally, emotionally and financially for the pet. Before you embark on this journey of raising your pet, it is important to evaluate your resources and make sure that you are ready for the pet. You should also evaluate the practical side of things. It is important that you know that the cost of bringing up a Pacman frog might be more than the cost you would have to encounter while raising a dog or a cat.

It is important to have a thorough understanding about the animal. Spend some time to know everything about the Pacman frog. This will help you know your pet better. The more you know about your pet, the better bond you will form with him. Whenever you get a pet home, you have to make sure that you are all ready for the responsibilities ahead. A pet is like a family member. This is the basic requirement to domesticate an animal. It is more than important that you take care of all the responsibilities for the animal.

If you wish to raise a Pacman frog as a pet, there are many things that you need to keep in mind. It can get very daunting for a new owner. Because of the lack of information, you will find yourself getting confused as to what should be done and what should be avoided. You might be confused and scared, but there is no need to feel so confused. After you learn about the Pacman frogs, you will know how adorable they are. You should equip yourself with the right knowledge.

Once you form a relationship with the Pacman frog, it gets better and easier for you as the owner. The pet will grow up to be friendly and adorable. He or she will also value the bond as much as you do. This will be good for the pet and also for you as the pet owner in the long run.

If you are in two minds about whether you need a Pacman frog or not, then this book will make it simpler for you. You should objectively look at the various advantages and disadvantages of owning a Pacman frog. This will help you to make your decision.

Here you can expect to learn the pet's basic behavior, eating habits, shelter requirements, grooming and training techniques among other important aspects. In short, the book will help you to be a better owner by learning everything about the animal. This will help you form an everlasting bond with the pet.

Chapter 1: Understanding the Pacman frog

The word Pacman frog is derived from a Latin word. The Pacman frog is also referred to as the South American horned frog because of their typical round shape and a very large mouth.

The domestic Pacman frog belongs to the weasel family of Ceratophyrs. They are also called ornato. The weasel family has many other members such as otters, minks and also the black-footed Pacman frog, which is an endangered species.

Pacman frogs are very beautiful to look at. They are very small in size. They weigh around 1-5 pounds. The Pacman frog will grow up to an average size of 5-7 inches. The length would be around 6 inches. Another interesting thing about the Pacman frog is that they can be found in different colors, such as cinnamon, sable and green.

Earlier, people hesitated to domesticate these beautiful animals. The main reason for this was that not much information was available about these animals. People had too many doubts and there was no source to clear these doubts.

But now, it has become easier for people to learn more about these animals and domesticate them. The adorable Pacman frogs are slowly becoming the most sought after pets.

1. Scientific classification

Kingdom – The Animalia

Phylum – The Chordata

Class – The Amphibia

Order – The Anura

Family – The Ceratophryidae

Genus – The Ceratophrys

Species – the M putorius

Sub species – The M p Furo

Being a member of the Ceraphyrs, the Pacman frog is a close relative of the weasel. There are many studies that have proven that the basic nature of the Pacman frog has some similarities with other members of Amphibia.

2. Domestic Pacman frog

The domestic Pacman frog is not a wild animal. There is evidence that proves that these animals have been domesticated for more than a thousand years now. They are domesticated all over the world. Their characteristics help them to be great domestic pets.

Most people believe that the domestic Pacman frog belongs to the class of rodents. This is not true. The Pacman frog is a descendant of South American frogs.

However, the domestic Pacman frog will have characteristics that are unique to them and will make them different from their ancestors. For example, the Pacman frog will enjoy social circles, which is not a characteristic that the ancestors will exhibit.

In the past, domestic Pacman frogs were also considered as working Pacman frogs. It is known that they are still used in UK to guard barns. These Pacman frogs help the owners to get rid of rodents. Pacman frogs were also known to scare off animals such as rabbits from their hiding areas.

If you are planning to bring a Pacman frog home, then you should know that these animals love to sleep. You might be surprised to learn that these animals can sleep 13-15 hours a day. The Pacman frog feels the most energetic and active during the late evening and also morning time.

The Pacman frog is naturally very fond of tunneling. They will always be on the lookout to dig a tunnel. When it comes to sleeping, the animal will prefer a safe, dark and enclosed area. This gives a feeling of security to the pet.

These animals are attention-seeking animals. If they are not sleeping, they will want to play with you. You should note that you can't keep them in a cage for too long.

They get depressed and stressed when they are lonely for too long, so as a prospective owner you should get ready to pamper the pet a lot.

3. Life span

A Pacman frog has a life span of 3-7 years. However, there have been instances where Pacman frogs have lived longer than their average life span.

The key is to provide them with the right environment and also the right nutrition. This will help them to grow, stay healthy and live longer.

It is also important to note that Pacman frogs are susceptible to various disease-causing viruses and bacteria. Once a Pacman frog gets a dangerous and life threatening disease, it can be very difficult to cure him.

A pet Pacman frog will require you to pay a lot of attention to its health, be it vaccination or health care. The pet will definitely live longer if you make sure that you do all that is necessary for its health.

4. Pacman frogs in their natural habitat

In their natural habitat, the Pacman frogs will be found together in groups. Such groups of Pacman frogs are referred to as a business. The young Pacman frog is often referred to as a kit. While the female Pacman frog is often called a Jill, a male Pacman frog is called a hob.

These Pacman frogs are carnivorous by nature. They love their meat and live on a meat diet. It is known that earlier Pacman frogs would eat only meat. Their main food consisted of small animals, such as rabbits and mice.

The Pacman frog has a very different digestive system. The digestive tract of the animal is very small. This arrangement has an effect on the food the Pacman frog eats and the Pacman frog's health in general. The Pacman frog has a high metabolism. While it can digest food faster than most animals, it can't digest many kinds of food.

A Pacman frog will have a scent gland. This will be located near the anus of the animal. The scent gland is used generally when the animal wishes to establish a territory.

They will also use it when they are scared of an impending danger. If the Pacman frog is neutered or spayed, then he is unable to use the scent gland.

Please note that although there are female Pacman frogs, we will refer to them as "he" for ease.

5. Dentition

The Pacman frog is known to have sharp teeth. A person who has been bitten by a Pacman frog will tell you this. There are basically four types of teeth in the Pacman frogs. Different types of teeth serve different purposes for the Pacman frog.

There are twelve teeth in the front that are called incisors. The primary purpose of these teeth is grooming. They are located between other types of teeth that are called canine and are very small in size.

The second types of teeth are called canines. These are very sharp and are basically used to tear apart the animal's prey. These are four in number.

The animal uses the pre molars to chew the food that they eat. These pre molar teeth are twelve in number. These teeth can be found behind canines and on the side of the Pacman frog's mouth.

Pacman frogs have a special kind of teeth to crush their food at the back of their mouth. These are called the molars and are six in number, with four being on the bottom and two of them being on the top.

6. Neutering or spaying

When you domesticate an animal, it also concerns you to understand its breeding cycles. As an owner, you need to make a decision whether you would want your pets to have progenies or not. This should be a well thought out decision, so that you can take the required actions.

These Pacman frogs are often neutered or spayed by the owners or the breeders. The neutered male Pacman frog is referred to as a gib and the spayed female Pacman frog is referred to as a sprite. Neutering or spaying is an important part of Pacman frog domestication.

When you are sure that you don't want your female Pacman frog to breed, it is better to spay the animal before it is too late. Similarly, neuter the male Pacman frog if you don't want breeding. Many breeders sell Pacman frogs after neutering or spaying the Pacman frogs.

It should also be understood that neutering or spaying the domestic Pacman frog will have its consequences on the Pacman frog. It is better to understand these consequences, talk to the veterinarian about them and be prepared for them.

When a female Pacman frog is not spayed, you will have to breed it. In case you are unable to do so, there will be health complications with the Pacman frog. The female Pacman frog could suffer from aplastic anemia.

7. Breeding in Pacman frogs

A female Pacman frog will get sexually matured by the age of about four months. On the other hand, the male Pacman frog will reach sexual maturity when he is six to nine months. If you wish to breed Pacman frogs at home, then you will have to be prepared for this task.

It will not be as simple as breeding a male and female animal. The Pacman frogs can acquire diseases if the wrong parents are mated. Closely related Pacman frogs should never be mated if you wish to keep the progeny healthy.

You will be required to get your female and male Pacman frogs tested for their genes to establish whether they can be successfully mated or not. It is better to discuss this in detail with your vet.

If you are planning to breed your male and female Pacman frog at home, you should be on the lookout for the signs that show that the Pacman frogs are ready.

It is said that the first spring after a Pacman frog's birth is the season for its mating. The days will get longer and warmer during this time. The first telltale sign that Pacman frogs are ready is that they secrete an odor and their skin becomes shiny because of the secretion.

The female Pacman frog should be four months of age whereas male Pacman frog should be at least six months of age. The female will have a discharge from her vagina and her vulva will also be swollen.

The male Pacman frog (hob) will be ready when his testicles enlarge and are visibly drooped from his body. The hob will also use his oil and urine to mark his territory. You might even see him rolling in his own urine. Once you are sure that the female and the hob are ready for mating, keep them in a single cage.

You should be ready to see some violent mating, which will not be a great sight. There will be a lot of dragging, wrestling and noise making. The male will bite the female on her neck so that she secretes her eggs.

The actual mating might take many hours or even many sessions. You should be prepared for this. This is normal, so there is nothing to worry about.

After the process, keep them in separate cages and observe your female Pacman frog for signs of conceiving. The first sign will be that she will gain weight and will also pull her own fur from her body and tail. She will also make noises.

However, sometimes the increase in weight can happen because of various hormones, so you should keep a check on her. She will eat more as the pregnancy approaches. An ultra sound can confirm the pregnancy. In case of a miscarriage, you can try to mate them again.

8. Legal regulations

When you are studying domestic Pacman frogs closely, it is important to understand the legal regulations that govern them. This will help you to know how easy it is for you domesticate the Pacman frog in your country.

- Brazil: If someone in Brazil wishes to domesticate these animals, then it possible with a few legalities. It is imperative to get the Pacman frogs sterilized. In addition, you will also be required to get the Pacman frog a microchip identification chip.

- New Zealand: Since 2002, New Zealand has made it illegal to breed and sell these animals. If you wish to domesticate a Pacman frog in New Zealand, you will have to go through various legalities to make this possible.

- Japan: Certain places in Japan make it very simple for owners to domesticate the Pacman frogs, for there are no restrictions. Yet some areas will require you to register yourself and the Pacman frog with the local body in your area.

- Australia: There are some places in Australia that allow the domestication of Pacman frogs. They may require you to have a legal license to domesticate them. There are some places where the keeping of these animals is illegal. For example, Queensland bans the domestication of Pacman frogs.

- United States: Earlier, the United States had banned the keeping and breeding of Pacman frogs, but as the Pacman frogs became popular in the late eighties and early nineties, the laws were changed in many places. Many places such as California still don't allow the domestication of Pacman frogs. Many military bases have banned Pacman frogs in their areas.

9. Things to know before you buy the Pacman frog

It is better that you plan the costs that you will incur while raising the Pacman frog well in advance. This planning will help you to avoid any kind of disappointment that you might face when there are some payments that need to be made. It is better if you plan these costs well in advance, so that you don't get in a mess at the later stage.

Before you are all set to buy the Pacman frog and domesticate him, it is also important that you work on all the costs that will go into raising the animal. This section will help you in understanding what you can expect in terms of costs when you are planning to bring a Pacman frog into your household.

In the very beginning, you need money to buy the Pacman frog. Once you have spent money on buying the animal, you should be ready to spend more money. You can expect to spend money on the shelter, healthcare and food of the animal.

While there are certain costs that will remain fixed, you will also have to be prepared for unexpected costs once in a while. You have to be ready to bear various costs continuously over the years. Being well prepared is the best way to go about things.

There are basically two kinds of costs that you will be looking to incur, which are as follows:

The one-time or initial costs: The initial costs are the costs that you will have to bear in the very beginning of the process of domestication of the animal. This will include the one-time payment that you will give to buy the animal.

There are other costs that would come under this category. The initial costs that you will face when you have decided to domesticate a Pacman frog are the purchasing cost of the animal, the permits and the license cost, the vaccines, costs of food containers and the costs of the enclosure.

The regular or monthly costs: Even when you are done with the one-time payments, there are some other costs that you won't be able to avoid. These costs can be planned well in advance. You can maintain a journal to keep track of these costs.

The monthly costs are the costs that you will have to spend each month or once in few months to raise the Pacman frog. The costs will include the costs of the food requirements and health requirements of the pet.

The various regular veterinarian visits, the sudden veterinarian visits and replacement of things come under the monthly costs category.

The various costs you can expect

While you are all excited to domesticate the Pacman frog, you should also start planning for the costs that you will incur. You can expect to incur the following the costs:

Cost of buying the Pacman frog

The initial purchasing price of the Pacman frog could be higher when compared to the initial amount incurred in purchasing other regular animals. If spending high amounts of money is an issue with you, then you will have to think twice before purchasing this animal.

On the other hand, if spending money is not an issue, then you should understand the other important factors in raising a Pacman frog and accordingly make a decision.

If you are planning to buy a Pacman frog from a pet shop, then you can expect to pay somewhere around $100/£77.62. In general, the Pacman frog can be anything from $65/£50.45 to about $250/£194.05.

But this is only the purchasing price of the Pacman frog; you will have to pay for the vaccinations of the animal too. These vaccinations could be anywhere between $100/£77.62 to 400 $400/£310.48.

You should make sure that you get the Pacman frog medically tested before buying it. The examination and tests will also add to the initial price. You also have the option to adopt a Pacman frog. This will help you to avoid the initial purchasing price, though the other costs for raising the Pacman frog will remain essentially the same.

You should also understand that neutering and spaying the animal will also add on to the price. If the Pacman frog has already been neutered and spayed, the breeder will inform you about this.

Most breeders mark the neutered or spayed Pacman frogs by two dots near the ears. Good breeders will always make sure that the Pacman frogs that they are selling to you and other buyers are in the prime of their health.

They will take care of their vaccines and health in general. This again means that the breeder will charge more.

If your breeder has taken care of the initial doses of vaccines, then you should be fine with paying a little extra to this breeder because he/she has saved you from running around to get these important procedures done.

Cost of shelter

When you bring a pet home, you have to make the necessary arrangements to give it a comfortable home. The shelter of the animal will be his home, so it is important that you construct the shelter according to the animal's needs.

If the pet is not indoors, most likely he will be in his cage. If the cage is not comfortable, you will see your Pacman frog withdrawing from it. Therefore, it is important to make this one time investment in a way that is best for the Pacman frog.

The Pacman frog will require a good quality and comfortable cage as its home. The Pacman frog will spend a lot of time indoors, but you should buy a good cage for the animal to rest and sleep.

If their shelter is not comfortable, the pet will be restless all the time. Even if you construct a very basic cage for the animal, it should have the necessary comforts.

This is a one-time cost, so you should not try to save money by putting the pet's comfort at stake. The price of shelter will depend on the type of the shelter. You can expect to spend anywhere between $50/£38.81 to $500/£388.1 for the cage of the Pacman frog.

The cage should be accessorized well by you. The cage will require some basic stuff, such as bedding, hammocks and toys. The higher end cages will have tunnels to keep the pet occupied and happy.

These are the extra things that you will have to incur in addition to the basic price of the cage. This should be around $70/£54.33. Though they might not be necessary, these accessories will make the cage fun for the Pacman frog.

Cost of food

A domesticated Pacman frog will mostly be fed cat and kitten food. Pacman frogs are opportunistic animals, so it is important that they are served more food items apart from the basic kitten food. You might also have to include various supplements to give your pet overall nourishment.

This is a basic requirement of the pet that you can't evade. It is important that you understand the food requirements of your Pacman frog in the beginning, so that you can be prepared on the monetary front.

This is important because if the animal does not get all the appropriate nutrients in the right amount, his health will suffer, which again will be an extra cost for you. So, make sure that you provide all the necessary nutrients to your pet animal.

You should be prepared to spend about $20/£15.52 to $40/£31.05 on the diet of your pet every month. The will vary depending on various factors, such as the brand of products that you choose and also your exact location.

The kinds of food that you feed your pet will also affect the exact amount food that you encounter per month. You should remember that the more lax you are regarding the money that goes into food, the lesser the amount of money that would go into health care.

If your pet is well fed, it will not fall sick that often. This will automatically reduce the amount of money that you would have to spend on the veterinarian and medication.

Cost of health care

It is important to invest in the health of a pet animal. This is necessary because an unhealthy animal is the breeding ground of many other diseases in the home. Your pet might pass on the diseases to other pets if not treated on time. This means danger for the pets and also the members of the family.

You will have to take the Pacman frog to the veterinarian for regular visits. He will be able to guide you regarding any medications and vaccines that the pet may need.

It is advised that for the very first year of domestication, you are extra careful regarding the health of the animal.

You should also be prepared for unexpected costs, such as sudden illness or accidents. Healthcare is provided at different prices in different areas, so the veterinarian in your area could be costlier than the veterinarian in the nearby town.

You should work out all these things right in the beginning, so that you don't suffer any problems later. Realizing at a later stage that you can't keep the animal and giving it up is never a good idea.

Pacman frogs can get sick very easily. You will have to invest in their health care. They are susceptible to many diseases such as respiratory infections and Adrenal diseases.

You should understand that taking care of these animals will require special skills. You should make sure that the veterinarian that you consult for your pet Pacman frog is experienced in handling such animals.

You should also be prepared to spend more money on their health than what you would have spent on other pet animals. It is believed that you should have an extra $1000/£776.2 saved for your Pacman frog's emergencies. He might require an operation or surgery because of a disease.

You will have to spend money on getting the vaccines for the Pacman frog. These vaccines are critical to save the pet from diseases and deficiencies at a later stage, so make sure that you don't miss them.

The Pacman frog will require vaccines against rabies and some other diseases. There are many breeders that take care of the early vaccines of the pet before giving it to the new owners.

You should talk to your breeder regarding this. The breeder might include the money spent on vaccines in the final price that he might charge for the animal. You should also keep a track of the vaccines, so that you don't miss any.

Other costs

Although the main costs that you will encounter while raising your pet have already been discussed, but there will be some extra things that you will have to take care of. Most of these are one-time costs only.

You will have to spend money to buy stuff such as Pacman frog bedding, accessories, food and water bowls, and toys for the pet.

You can expect to spend some $200/£155.24 on these things. The exact amount will depend on the wear and tear and the quality of the products. In order to keep track of things, you should regularly check the various items in the cage of the pet.

If you think that something needs to be repaired or replaced, you should go ahead and do it.

10. Housing of the Pacman frog

Housing a pet is a very big responsibility. The animal needs to feel safe and comfortable. If you are unable to provide the pet with the same then you will only make the life of the pet difficult. This in turn will make your life difficult.

You should make all the possible arrangements so that the pet gets all the necessary comfort in your home. Learn about the natural surroundings of the pet. This will help you to create a happy space for the animal.

There are many people that forget that a pet animal is a family member. Just like you would do everything to make the life easier for a family member, you should do the same for your pet animal.

The frog can't talk and ask you for all that it needs. You need to be proactive and do all that is possible to make the life of the pet easier.

There are many people that believe that housing a frog will be a very difficult task. People think that the conditions required for the Pacman frog would be difficult to maintain at a human house, but this is not true.

You would be happy to learn here that it is easy to house a Pacman frog. It is much simpler than housing many other popular house pets.

This section will help you to understand what needs to be done to make sure that the pet is having a comfortable stay in your home. You will learn about all the dos' and don'ts that you need to follow.

Having said that, it should be noted here that you don't need to feel intimidated. A pet is kept in the home for joy. It is more than important that you maintain this joy while taking care of the pet.

Don't make the entire process a task. This will not help you or the pet. Rather, be happy and joyful and do all that needs to be done for the pet to be kept safe and healthy.

How to house more than one Pacman frog

In their natural habitat, the Pacman frog is usually found in a colony. There are numerous colonies consisting of many Pacman frogs.

Because they are used to being in groups, you can easily house more than one Pacman frog in your home. The major problem is that you will have to get used to the hissing sounds of the frogs.

The Pacman frog is a social creature. It will display behavior that will make it suitable to live in groups. This is great for people who are looking to house multiple frogs.

If you are looking to house multiple Pacman frogs, there are few things that you need to keep in mind. The gender of the insects would need to be considered. You can't house them randomly because that can lead to many issues.

Housing multiple male frogs

Female Pacman frogs have a liking and attraction to dominant male members. Dominant male members in a territory tend to have a very loud and aggressive kind of hissing.

The males are very aggressive to each other when it comes to marking their territory. They push one another to show the opponent how strong they are.

It is not surprising that the frogs are capable of hurting each other. Many male frogs hurt each other while they are deeply engrossed in these kinds of territorial fights, which are very aggressive.

This makes it very important that too many male frogs are not housed together because this will create problems for the less dominant male frogs. It will also be unpleasant for your family to keep seeing the frogs fighting.

It should be noted here that because the male members can fight over establishing a territory, it is not that the males should never be housed together. The less dominant one will lose but will not be severely harmed. You can expect a few hurts and bruises.

Housing multiple female frogs

If you wish to house multiple female frogs, then you should know that the female frogs are pretty docile to each other.

The female frogs don't indulge in fights to establish territory because that is the job of the male members. They females are social and easy going.

You can expect your female frogs to indulge in hissing from time to time. The hissing will not be as aggressive and loud as the hissing of the male frogs. It will be much softer.

The females can hiss alone or in a group as communal hissing. This shouldn't be very disturbing for you and your family, though it is better to be prepared.

These simple points should be kept in mind when you are looking to house multiple frogs in your home. You will not face too much problem when looking to house multiple frogs in your home.

Housing female and male frogs together

If you are thinking about housing female and male frogs together, then you can easily do it. The male and female frogs can co-exist happily.

This can particularly be a good idea if you are interested in mating male and female frogs.

Female Pacman frogs have a liking and attraction towards the dominant male members. The males will fight over dominance with each other so that they can attract the female frog.

Dominant male members in a territory tend to have a very loud and aggressive kind of hissing. The weaker ones will not be able to show much power and will also hiss in softer tones when compared to the dominant male frogs.

11. Bringing home a healthy Pacman frog

A major concern that many prospective owners and buyers of the Pacman frog is how to make sure that the animal that they are getting home is healthy.

It is extremely critical that you get a healthy Pacman frog to your home because once you get an unhealthy kit you will only make things worse for yourself and the pet.

In the excitement of getting a new pet, you shouldn't forget the basic checks that you need to do before bringing the Pacman frog home. The last thing that anyone would expect after finding a breeder and getting an animal is that it is not in good health.

You will not know how to care for the sick pet. The pet's health will deteriorate. You will be spending thousands of dollars just on the health of the animal.

The following pointers will help you to make sure that your future pet is in the prime of its health:

- It is very important to bring a healthy pet to your home. You should definitely avoid bringing an injured animal home.

- If you are buying an older Pacman frog, you need to be all the more vigilant because they could carry some infections.

- First and foremost, you should check the health care card of the animal that you wish to buy. All good breeders will maintain a health card, which will have all the details of past diseases and infections. This health card will also help you to understand the vaccines cycle of the animal.

- You will be able to understand which vaccines have been completed and which ones are due.

- It is always better to buy a Pacman frog whose vaccines have not been cancelled or missed.

- It is important that you closely examine your prospective pet. You should look for any abrasions on his skin.

- His skin should not be torn or bruised from anywhere.

- You should make it a point to check the body temperature of the Pacman frog. The body temperature should be normal. If the Pacman frog is too cold or too hot to touch, then there is some problem with its health.

- You should closely look for any kind of injuries. If you find anything that does not seem normal, then you need to discuss it with the breeder.

- The Pacman frog should not have any broken limbs. You should be able to check this manually. You should look for any hanging limbs. A hanging head or limb could mean that the pet is severely injured.

- Carefully inspect the tail and stomach area also. There should be no abrasions.

- It is important that the Pacman frog is devoid of any infections or diseases when you bring him home.

- It is advisable to take the help of a qualified veterinarian to be sure of the kit's health conditions. He or she will be the best judge of his condition. A good vet will always guide you in the right direction for the Pacman frog.

- You should discuss at length the concerns that you have regarding the Pacman frog.

- You should follow all the instructions that the doctor gives you because they will be for the benefit of the animal.

- You should only keep the Pacman frog if you are convinced that you will be able to care for the little animal.

- After you have brought the Pacman frog home, you should keep him isolated to keep an eye on him.

- You should allow him inside the house only after a few days of checking if everything is normal with the Pacman frog.

- In case of any issues, you should consult the vet and/or the breeder.

12. Handling the Pacman frog

When you keep a pet, handling the pet is one of the main concerns in the minds of the owners. Nobody wants to buy a pet that can't be handled.

This section will help you to understand how you can handle your Pacman frog in the best possible way.

There are some Pacman frog enthusiasts that are just beginning their hobby to keep different kinds of Pacman frogs but are confused as to which ones to keep. The Pacman frog is the safest bet for them.

Such people should start from a relatively easier species such as the Pacman frog, and then move to other species. This is how simple it is to handle a Pacman frog.

There are many people who fear that they might harm the pet out of inexperience. You don't need to be afraid for this. Pacman frog has a hard exoskeleton, which gives the pet a good structure.

The exoskeleton makes sure that the frog is protected against external harms. You can lift the frog without the fear of harming it.

The Pacman frog is larger in size when you compare it to other Pacman frog species. This also makes it easier to handle the Pacman frog. The larger the frog, the easier it is to handle.

While it is easy to handle the Pacman frog, it does not mean that you can be extremely careless when handling the pet. You can't throw the pet here and there. You have to make sure that you are as careful as possible.

The Pacman frog is your responsibility, and you should be able to do everything to make sure that the Pacman frog is safe and sound in your care.

We will discuss some tips and tricks to make sure that the pet is safe when you are handling it. You should also make sure that all the family members understand the importance of handling a pet well.

If you are unable to do so, you can harm the pet. You can also scare the pet. He might get aggressive near you if he feels that he is not safe around you.

The following guidelines will come in handy while handling the Pacman frog:

- Make sure the kids of the family are not alone with the frog. Even if the kid does not mean harm, he or she can accidentally hurt the frog. This can be very serious, so it is better that the children are accompanied by an adult when they are handling the frog.

-

- You should never startle the frog when he is resting on your hand. This can cause him to drop on the ground, which again can be very serious for the pet.

-

- When you are holding the frog in your hands, make sure that the grip of the hands is just right. You don't want your hands to be too tight or too lose. If the grip is too tight, you can hurt the pet, and if it is too loose, he can drop from your hands.

-

- When you are handling the frog, make sure that the distance between the frog and the ground is not too high. This eliminates the risk of the frog falling very hard and hurting himself. This rule should be followed sincerely when you are still learning how to handle the frog.

- You need to be extra careful during the first few days when the pet is not used to you and you are not used to the pet. It is important to give each other time.

- Never apply too much force to pick up the frog. Be as gentle as possible. A sudden movement from your side can harm the Pacman frog.

How to pick up the frog

It is important that you pick up the frog in an easy and comfortable way without stressing and without hurting the frog. To pick up the Pacman frog, gently place your fingers around the thorax and lift it gently. The thorax is the section that is quite hard and is behind the head area of the Pacman frog.

Never apply too much force to pick up the frog. Be as gentle as possible.

Chapter 2: Owning a Pacman frog

If you wish to own a Pacman frog or even if you already own one, it is important to understand the basic characteristics of the animal. You should know what you can expect from the animal and what you can't.

This will help you to tweak the way you behave with the Pacman frog in the household, which in turn will help to build a strong bond between the Pacman frog and you.

Pacman frogs are known to be very loyal animals. If they establish trust with you, they will always remain loyal to you. This is a great quality to have in a domesticated animal.

Along with being loyal, they are also known to possess great intelligence.

When the Pacman frog is in a happy mood, he will jump around the entire space. His unique ways and antics will leave you and the entire family laughing. If you have had a bad day, your pet will surely help you to release all the tension and enjoy life.

They are also very entertaining and playful. You can expect the entire household to be entertained by the unique gimmicks and pranks of the Pacman frog. If you are looking for a pet that is affectionate, lovable and fun, then the Pacman frog is the ideal choice for you, as they won't disappoint you.

In spite of all the qualities of the Pacman frog, it is often termed as a high maintenance pet. If you are still contemplating whether you wish to buy a Pacman frog or not, then it is important that you understand all about the maintenance of the pet, so that you can make the right choice for yourself.

1. Advantages and disadvantages of domesticating Pacman frogs

If you are in two minds whether you need a Pacman frog or not, then this section will make it simpler for you. You should objectively look at the various advantages and disadvantages of owning a Pacman frog. This will help you to make your decision.

It is important that you understand that owning any pet will have its advantages and disadvantages. You should see whether with all its pros and cons, the animal fits well into your household. A few advantages and disadvantages of the domestication of Pacman frogs have been discussed in this section. If you are a prospective buyer, then this section will help you to make a wise decision.

There are people who are impressed by the adorable looks of the Pacman frog. They think that this reason is enough to domesticate the animal. They believe that just because the pet is tiny, it wouldn't require any maintenance. This is not true.

The domestication of a Pacman frog has its unique challenges and issues. If you are not ready for these challenges, then you are not ready to domesticate the animal. Once you understand the areas that would require extra work from your side, you will automatically give your very best in those areas.

If you have already bought or adopted a Pacman frog, even then this section will help you. The list of pros and cons of Pacman frogs will help you to prepare yourself for the challenges that lie ahead of you. This list will help you to be a better parent to the pet and to form an ever-lasting bond with your beloved pet.

Advantages of domesticating a Pacman frog

If you are still not sure about adopting or buying a Pacman frog, then you should know that there are many pros of domesticating a Pacman frog. They are loved by their owners and their families because of some amazing qualities that they possess.

The various advantages of domesticating a Pacman frog are as follows:

- The size of the Pacman frog makes it an ideal choice as a pet. They weigh between 1 to 5 pounds, which makes them very light in comparison to many other commonly domesticated animals.

- Their looks make them adorable and cute to look at. They are loved by one and all. Who wouldn't want to have a pet that is beautiful to look at?

- People who love pets that can be lifted and cuddled will love the Pacman frog. A Pacman frog will allow you to lift it and play with it.

- This pet will be the center of affection for all the family members and also for each and every visitor of the house.

- Pacman frogs are known to be very loyal kinds of animals. They will love your presence around them and will show you that they love you in their own unique ways.

- Pacman frogs are also known to possess great intelligence. You should be prepared to witness their intelligent antics and gimmicks.

- If you care well for the pet, he will also respond in a very positive way. When the Pacman frog is in a happy mood, he will jump around the entire space. His unique ways and antics will leave you laughing.

- If there are kids in your home, then they will fall in love with this pet. However, you should monitor the interaction of the kids with the pet. This is important to keep everyone safe and sound.

- The Pacman frog is a very active and energetic animal when it is awake. It will keep itself happy and entertained. You will not have to worry much about the pet. In fact, this animal will be really fun to be around for all the family members. The Pacman frog will entertain you and your family and will everyone happy with its antics.

- These pets sleep a lot. They will sleep most of the time, which gives you a lot of free time to do whatever you want to do.

- One of your main concerns could be the diet of the pet. Even if you love your pet dearly, you would want to avoid any hassle while feeding the pet. You might not have the time to prepare special food all the time. The Pacman frog can be served meat with some store bought Pacman frog food or kitten food. There are easily available food items to ensure that the right nutrition is given to your pet, so diet should not be too much of a worry.

- Pacman frogs don't overeat, so you don't have to worry about this. You can leave food in the container and the Pacman frog will eat as much is required. They are used to eating several small meals.

- Pacman frogs can be trained against nipping. You can also litter train them. You can teach them some easy tricks to have more fun with them.

- A very important point to note here is that their demeanor will depend a lot on how they are raised. The preparation has to begin right from the start. You can't expect them to suddenly become friendly after years of wrong treatment. If they are raised to be social, they will be very social.

- The animal will secrete a gland that will make him smell when he is frightened and alarmed. However, if the pet is neutered or spayed, there will be no stinking and dirty smells. This can be a great relief for many people, because who wants a pet who smells all the time?

- Pacman frogs live in groups in their natural environment. This makes them tolerant towards other Pacman frogs. The Pacman frogs will wrestle and play with each other. There is a very slight possibility that they will not get along.

- Pacman frogs have a fairly long life, if they are taken care of. You can make a strong emotional bond with your pet and can enjoy the fruits of the bond for years to come.

Disadvantages of domesticating a Pacman frog

While you have studied the advantages of domesticating a Pacman frog, it is also important to learn about the various disadvantages that come with it. Everything that has merits will also have some down sides, and you should be prepared for this.

The adorable and friendly animal has his own set of challenges when it comes to domesticating them. It is important to understand these disadvantages so that you can be better prepared for them. Here are the disadvantages of raising a Pacman frog:

- The Pacman frogs are very energetic by nature. This behavior could be difficult for a first time owner.

- These animals have a very unique temperament, and it would require patience from your side to understand this kind of temperament.

- These animals sleep a lot. Though this can be an advantage for you, if you want a pet that will play with you all day, then you are in for a loss. The Pacman frog will play with you when it wants to.

- Pacman frogs can't see very well. The Pacman frog can get hurt if it is too dark because of their weak eyesight.

- These animals are known to eat smaller but very frequent meals. So, you have to make sure that the Pacman frog has something to eat every 2-3 hours. Such maintenance could be difficult for some people.

- They get sick very easily. A lot of care has to be taken to ensure that they maintain good health.

- The Pacman frog has a habit of nipping. This is a habit that helps them to interact with other Pacman frogs, but they can nip you also. Nipping can hurt you, but you can train the Pacman frog against such behavior.

- The food that you serve them might be easily available, but the right brands might not be too cheap.

- They are definitely not suitable for someone who is looking for a quiet and calm pet. They are energetic, will run around and will also make noises.

- Because of his energy levels, the Pacman frog can run into things and can get hurt very easily.

- Pacman frogs are known to have very sharp teeth that can hurt small children. So, you need to make sure that the children are never left alone with the pet.

- They are so small that you can lose them if you don't keep track of what they are doing. This is very important. If the Pacman frog is lost, it is almost impossible to find it. He will not be able to find his way back to the house.

- The Pacman frog loves to dig in the ground. In fact, the pet will try to dig everywhere. If the Pacman frog is left on its own, he might try to dig in your sofas, beds, etc.

- The pet also loves to chew. They can chew away at all your furniture and bedding.

- The animal seeks a lot of attention. The Pacman frog is a kind of pet that will require you to pamper him a lot.

- The pet can get stressed and depressed if he is left lonely for longer durations. You can't leave him in the cage for too long.

- The cost that you will incur while buying and raising is more when compared to other pets, such as the dog or cat.

- You will have to spend a lot of money on the vaccinations and healthcare of the Pacman frog.

- If spending too much money is an issue with you, then you will have to think twice before purchasing the animal.

- You should also understand the various other costs that you will encounter while raising your pet. You will have to spend a lot of money on their health.

2. Introducing the Pacman frog to a new Pacman frog

There are many people who want to keep more than one Pacman frog in their home, but are scared of the consequences. What if the Pacman frogs don't get along? What if the older Pacman frog gets insecure? If you too are having the same set of questions, then this particular section will help to clear most of your doubts.

To begin with, you should know that keeping more than one Pacman frog in a household is not a bad idea. In most cases, the Pacman frogs give each other company. A Pacman frog can get severely stressed of he is lonely.

If you have made the decision to buy a new Pacman frog at a later stage, you will have to take certain precautions. It is always better if you get young kits of about the same age if you are sure about keeping more than one Pacman frog. These kits will grow up together and it will be easier for them to get along.

If you have a Pacman frog that is very old and sick, it can be very difficult for him to adjust with a new Pacman frog. On the other hand, if your Pacman frog is healthy, you can introduce him to a new Pacman frog by taking certain precautions.

If you think that you can bring a Pacman frog home and just leave him with the older Pacman frog, then it will get very difficult for you. The older pet could have territorial issues that you will have to address. In addition, the new Pacman frog could carry some disease-causing bacteria or virus. You will have to make sure that the new Pacman frog does not pass on these to the older one.

The first thing that you need to do when you are planning to bring a new Pacman frog home is to get another cage for the Pacman frog. You can get a simple cage for him because this will only be his temporary home. You should keep the new Pacman frog in this cage for a few weeks.

Keeping the new Pacman frog in an isolated cage is important for both the old and the new frog. The new frog will get some time to get adjusted to the new environment around him. If he is a kit, he will need some space and time to understand his surroundings.

The old Pacman frog, on the other hand, will be protected from any disease that the new Pacman frog might be carrying. The Pacman frog that is bought from the breeder could be a carrier of some disease or virus.

It is important that you keep the cage of the new Pacman frog away from the old Pacman frog. They should ideally be in separate rooms. It is critical that you observe a quarantine period of at least two weeks. These two weeks will help you to establish whether your new pet Pacman frog is healthy or not.

It is important that the new Pacman frog has had all his vaccines on time. Before you bring him home, you should make sure that you check the health card of the Pacman frog. This will help you to understand the health condition of the new pet that you want to bring home.

It is known that Pacman frogs can transmit ECE to each other. There is nothing much you can do in this case, but you can definitely prevent your Pacman frog from acquiring a disease from the new Pacman frog. With the passage of time, if you witness your new pet to be unwell, you should take him to the vet.

After the passage of the first few weeks, you can be sure that the new Pacman frog is not carrying any disease. Now, it is time to slowly introduce the pets to each other, but this has to be done in stages.

If you think that the two of them can be put together and they'll suddenly become the best of buddies, this is not going to happen.

You should understand that the older Pacman frog is already used to a certain lifestyle. He is used to a way of living and also to the people and pets around him. If suddenly a new pet walks in, it will get difficult for him on various levels. He will try to fight it out with the new Pacman frog to establish his supremacy.

This fight for survival and supremacy will not only strain the relationship of the pets, but will also lead to a lot of stress in their lives. As the owner, it is your responsibility to avoid any such situation where your pets have to go through unnecessary pressure and stress.

To make the transition easier for both the Pacman frogs, you should begin by introducing them to each other's smell. After the first few weeks of isolating them, bring their cages closer. You can place the cage of the new Pacman frog next to the cage of the older one in a way that they can see each other and smell each other.

It is important to keep the Pacman frogs in this arrangement for a few days so that they get used to each other's smell. Another trick that you apply is that you can exchange the bedding of the two Pacman frogs after a few days. This is a technique that will help them to identify each other's smell.

Once the Pacman frogs are okay with each other's smell, you can be sure that it'll get better from there. Give them a few days, and during this time don't bring them physically in one area. Just keep them around in separate cages.

Once you see them acknowledging each other, you know it is time to introduce them in a more intimate way. You can now bring them together in an open space. By now, they know of each other's presence in the house.

You will find them smelling and sniffing one another. This is the Pacman frogs' way of introducing themselves. You need to supervise such meetings. Though they will not harm each other, but you shouldn't leave them alone. Do this for a few days.

The introduction period could extend up to many days and weeks. You might also find your Pacman frogs wrestling with each other. This, again, is a very normal behavior in Pacman frogs, so you shouldn't be surprised. Wrestling is a way to establish who the dominant one in the pack is.

They will nip each other, drag each other and flip each other. This would be accompanied by hissing sounds. You should not interfere in the wrestling bout, unless things get very serious. If you see a Pacman frog bleeding or being too stressed and scared, then you know that it is time to intervene.

You should also know that the age of the pets will also determine how well they get along. It is always easier for younger Pacman frogs to get along with each other. If the older Pacman frog at your home has been there for many years, he will take a lot of time to accept the new Pacman frog.

If the new Pacman frog is very young, you can wait for a few months before you introduce him to the older Pacman frog. This is the best for both of them. You can expect your pets to get jealous when they see you spending more time with the other one.

To balance things out, you should try to spend time with both and should also be very loving and encouraging in your words. They will sense your tone and love. You have to do this so that the Pacman frogs don't feel lonely and left out.

If the Pacman frogs seem to enjoy playing together, they will slowly start getting along. A strong indication that the pets are comfortable with each other is when they are curling up together. You might find them all curled up and sleeping next to each other. This is when you can put the Pacman frogs together in a cage.

However, even this task should be done in small steps. Initially, keep them together only for some time. Then, slowly increase it. Add news toys to the cage and observe the Pacman frogs' reactions. Remove the toys that seem to create tension between the two Pacman frogs.

In most cases, the Pacman frogs will eventually get along, but if your Pacman frogs are brutal towards each other and refuse to get along even after multiple trials, then you know that they need to be away from each other.

If you notice blood shed each time they are together, then this is not a good sign. In such a case, you are advised to have two separate cages for the Pacman frog.

3. Pacman frog vaccination

It is important that you understand everything about Pacman frog vaccination. This will help you keep all the vaccination doses on time. Make sure that you never miss a dose.

The breeder should also give you the health update of the Pacman frog when you purchase him. You should know every little detail about your pet.

Pacman frogs can get sick very easily and this makes it all the more important to do everything that would help them to be healthy. Your pet is at a high risk of canine distemper. It is extremely important to vaccinate the Pacman frog to eliminate this danger. This should be done when the Pacman frog is at the age of about eight weeks.

After this dose, it is important to give the Pacman frog a dose at eleven weeks and also fourteen weeks. Once this is done, you will have to make sure that the pet gets a dose every year.

This is very important to keep the pet Pacman frog safe. It is very important that you discuss the vaccination type with the veterinarian.

The Pacman frog should only be given a pure vaccine for only the specified disease. There will be no other vaccines for other conditions. It is important that the Pacman frog gets a pure vaccine for this condition. FerVac-D is known to be a pure vaccine, and this also has been certified and approved by USDA.

Just like a vaccine against canine distemper is needed, a vaccine against rabies is also essential. The first dose for the vaccine for the same should be given to the Pacman frog at the age of about sixteen weeks. After this initial dose, you should make sure that a dose for the vaccine is given once every year.

Make sure that you don't miss any doses for any vaccines that the Pacman frog requires. If your pet does not get the vaccines on time, there is a chance that he might acquire the disease. If your pet acquires rabies and the vaccines are not given to the pet, the state might decide to get the pet Pacman frog put down.

After your pet has been given a vaccine dose, he might feel a little lethargic and will want to rest and sleep. This is absolutely normal behavior, so you should allow your Pacman frog to rest. If you see any abnormal behavior or the Pacman frog getting sick, then you should take the Pacman frog to the veterinarian.

It is also important to keep some gap between two kinds of vaccines. You should keep a gap because this will prevent any negative reaction of the doses, and it will also be easier for the pet Pacman frog. You should discuss this point with the veterinarian and should plan the dates of various vaccines accordingly.

Your Pacman frog can also be at risk of heartworm, which is caused by mosquitoes. Pacman frogs spend very less time in open spaces and mostly stay indoors, but there is no way to ensure that your home has no mosquitoes.

If a mosquito bites the pet, and if the mosquito is the carrier of the infection, then your Pacman frog is at risk of heartworm. The best way to prevent this disease is to get the Pacman frog vaccinated against the infection. If you live in an area that has lot of mosquitoes, then it becomes all the more important to get this vaccination.

You should discuss your concerns with the veterinarian and ask him/her for the vaccination doses and details. Depending on the area and the prevalence of mosquitoes in the area, the doses will be decided.

You might even have to get a prevention dose every month for your pet. But, this is better than getting the infection because once the Pacman frog gets the infection it will be difficult to treat him.

Chapter 3: Decoding the Pacman frog's behavior

A Pacman frog is a small, naughty animal that will keep you busy and entertained by all its unique antics and mischiefs. It is said that each animal is different from the other. Each one will have some traits that are unique to him.

While you will learn about all the unique traits that your particular Pacman frog has by experiencing him and spending time with him, there are some traits that almost all Pacman frogs will exhibit. It is beneficial to know of these traits so that you are not taken off guard. You will be able to understand what is normal for this animal and what is not.

The following personality traits will help you to be better prepared for your pet Pacman frog:

1. Wrestling

If you are planning to domesticate more than one Pacman frog, then this is one antic that you will notice a lot in your Pacman frogs. Pacman frogs love to wrestle with each other. Actually, Pacman frogs are very joyful and playful, but they can be very rough with each other while playing.

The dominant Pacman frog will try his antics on the poor submissive one. You will find them making sounds of excitement. Don't worry because this is a very normal behavior in Pacman frogs. Do keep an eye on the Pacman frogs so that things don't get out of hand.

2. Alligator roll

This is a special kind of roll in which a Pacman frog holds another Pacman frog by his loose skin and rolls him over. This is a very common trait in Pacman frogs. If you are planning to have more than one Pacman frog at your home, you can expect to witness a lot of alligator rolls.

This technique is basically a way of establishing supremacy for a Pacman frog. A strong and dominant Pacman frog will get hold of the loose skin at the back of the submissive Pacman frog and roll him. There is nothing to worry about because such flips are generally not harmful and the Pacman frogs are just being playful.

If a Pacman frog is alone, he might just flip and roll on the floor to show that he is happy and playful. You should worry if the Pacman frog tries to try this on you. He might try to get hold of loose skin on you and might try to nip you and bite you. This can be painful for you, but you should know that this is a very normal thing for a Pacman frog and that you can nip train him.

3. Spotting a frightened and scared Pacman frog

It is easy to spot a scared Pacman frog. If you see your Pacman frog pushed up in a corner, you should know that something is not right. If he is making noises similar to a hiss then you should know that he is definitely scared.

It is important to know when your pet is scared so that you can comfort him and make him feel better. There are different ways to comfort different kinds of animals. For your Pacman frog, you just need to let him be.

Leave the pet alone, but be in the vicinity so that you can keep check on him. The Pacman frog is known to recover on its own. He will know when the danger that frightened him is no longer there, and this will help him to be normal. If you really wish to help then say a few kind words to your pet.

Don't make the mistake of taking him in your arms. This is not required right now. Just speak a few kind words to reinforce the fact that everything is fine and then just leave the Pacman frog for some time. This works for a scared Pacman frog.

It should also be noted here that there is another reason for a Pacman frog to curl into a corner. This could also mean that the Pacman frog wants to defecate. If you see your Pacman frog tucked up into a corner, look out for the possibility whether he is scared or not. If you don't hear him making noises or acting scared, then this means that he wants to defecate.

As soon as you have established that this is the reason for your pet to be in the corner, you should take him to a litter box. It should be noted that if you don't act immediately, your pet will defecate on your floor or carpet. He will not wait for you to act, so you need to be quick.

4. Puffy body

As explained earlier, a puffy body could mean that the Pacman frog is scared. A Pacman frog that has taken up a corner, has a puffy tail and is making noises is definitely scared, but there could also be other reasons for a puffy tail. A puffy tail would signify that either the Pacman frog is too excited or too scared.

If you see your Pacman frog jumping around having a puffy tail, you should immediately know that the pet is very excited. This could happen if the pet is in an area for the very first time. This could also happen if the pet is involved in very high intensity play. Some Pacman frogs get the puffy tail when they are let out during cool morning hours.

The puffy tail is also called the bottlebrush tail. The tail will basically look all puffed up. You can expect your Pacman frog to be all charged up like a rocket at this time. You will notice immense amounts of energy in him. He will dart from one end to another in seconds and you should just forget about catching up with him.

5. Dance of joy

A very popular and endearing trait of the Pacman frog is its dance of joy. When a Pacman frog is all excited, he will jump and flip and will dart from one side to another. You might see him jumping from the top of furniture. This is the dance of joy.

The Pacman frog might also emit certain kinds of sounds during this dance. This is a simple indication for you that the pet is very excited and happy and wants to play and have some fun with you.

A new owner might not take well to this unique way of displaying excitement. There are many owners and their family members who get scared after seeing the Pacman frog like this, but you should know that this behavior is completely normal and the Pacman frog will not harm you. He is just having fun and wants to include you in his fun.

6. War dance

The war dance is basically a set of movements that the Pacman frog displays when he is upset, frightened or angry. The movements could seem quite similar to the dance of joy to many people, but if you look closely, you will understand that the two are very different.

The key is to observe the body language of the pet Pacman frog. If the Pacman frog is sticking to a corner, is making noises, has a bent or arched back and has his fur standing, then the Pacman frog is definitely upset, angry or scared.

If the pet is not neutered, he will also emit a very filthy smell. This should be a clear indication that something is not right with the pet. The Pacman frog will pose like he is very strong and will be sticky to ward off the danger.

When you see a sad or angry Pacman frog, your first instinct as the parent would be to pick the pet up and calm him down. If you get over protective, he might just get irritated and might just bite you in frustration. You should say some kind and soothing words to the pet. When a pet Pacman frog is angry, he needs some time to calm down.

7. Chase

Chase is one of the favorite games of Pacman frogs. If you have more than one Pacman frog, you will often see them chasing each other. The pet will also try to get the attention of the owner either to chase him or to get chased by him.

Many new owners get scared when they see their pet all excited running around them. There is nothing to worry about because the pet is only trying to start a game of chase with you. You can take a long cloth such as a blanket or towel and run with it. Your Pacman frog will happily run after you.

If you are the one who is chasing the Pacman frog, then make sure that you maintain a good distance between you and the animal because these animals have another unique trait. The Pacman frog might just suddenly stop while running. If you are not careful, you might trample your pet Pacman frog, which is the last thing that you would want to do with your pet.

8. Digging

There are certain traits that are inborn in an animal. No matter how unwanted and troublesome that might seem to you, you have to get used to it. One such trait in the Pacman frog is digging.

While it is okay if they try to dig a blanket or the ground in the open yard, it can be troublesome if they try to dig their food. Many Pacman frogs will exhibit this nature. When you serve food to them in a food bowl, they will get all excited and will try to dig the food. This will not result in anything but a lot of mess.

As an owner, you can just ignore this habit because it comes naturally to him. Furthermore, the Pacman frog will eat the food that has fallen out of the food bowl. Many people might get disturbed by this habit, but it is better to just get used to it as soon as possible.

9. Tipping bowls

Another habit of the pet Pacman frog that could annoy you as the owner is the tipping of food and water bowls. This habit could also come as a shock to you. You might notice that the Pacman frog just flips the food container or the water container. It has nothing to do whether they like the food or not.

It is more like a signal to you that the Pacman frog is bored. If the Pacman frog is in the cage for too long, they can get lonely and bored. In their anger and boredom, they will just flip the container. You should make sure that the pet is not caged for too long so as to keep him away from loneliness.

Apart from being bored, there is another reason that could be behind this action. The animal loves to dig. Out of habit they dig and flip things around them. The Pacman frog also likes to play in water, especially shallow water. They also like to play with everything around them, so this could be their way of playing with the food and water.

There are a few tricks that you can employ to keep this behavior in check. You can't change the basic behavior of the Pacman frog, but you can work things around his behavior. For example, you should use heavy base containers for food and water so that the Pacman frog can't easily flip them.

You can also make use of extensions that keep the containers attached to the cage. This will also help to keep the containers in place. There is another trick that you can use to make the Pacman frog eat the food rather than play with it.

Sprinkle some water over the food in the food container. This will attract the Pacman frog. He will try to lick the water droplets and in the process will also eat some of the food. You should throw away this food if the Pacman frog does not eat it because food mixed with water will get spoilt easily.

10. Digging in the litter box

As you might have understood by now, the Pacman frog is very fond of digging up places. He might not leave the litter box. A Pacman frog in a litter box is not something very hygienic. You will have to adopt some tips to stop your Pacman frog from digging in the litter box.

If the box is very clean, it could be like an invitation to the Pacman frog to come and dig. You can try keeping some feces in the box, so that the Pacman frog stays away from it. When the Pacman frog approaches such a place, he will smell the stool. The smell will tell him that this place is to shit and not dig.

Another way to reduce the behavior of digging anywhere is to get a sand box for the Pacman frog. You will find it easily at the pet shop that houses Pacman frog related products. This box will give the Pacman frog a designated place to dig. This will reduce the impulse of the pet to dig any and every place.

11. Dooking

Dooking refers to the sounds that are made by the Pacman frogs when they are very happy. An excited Pacman frog will display its happiness by jumping around and also by making certain noises. Sometimes, these noises are very soft, and you will have to listen closely to even notice.

At other times, the ecstatic Pacman frog will make very loud noises. The dance of joy is often accompanied by dooking. You should not be scared of these noises because they are perfectly normal. You should pay more attention to your pet's moods and behavior to understand what kind of sounds it makes at different times.

12. Hissing

While dooking means that all is well with the pet, hissing is just the opposite. When the Pacman frog is frightened or angry, it will make noises like hissing. Again, you have to closely observe your pet to understand his moods and the accompanying sounds.

When you see a sad or angry Pacman frog, your first instinct as the parent would be to pick the pet up and calm him down. But, you are advised not to do so. When a pet Pacman frog is angry, he needs some time to calm down. If you get over protective, he might just get irritated and might just bite you in frustration.

You should say some kind and soothing words to the pet. Your tone will make him realize that you care for him. After that just leave the area. The Pacman frog needs some time. He will utilize this time and will cool down on his own.

Another point to be noted here is that an over excited Pacman frog might also make a similar noise. When two or more Pacman frogs are left to play with each other, they could emit a sound quite similar to hissing. It is important that you understand whether the pet is angry, scared or just having fun.

You can use a simple trick to know whether the pet is angry or not. You should pay attention to the Pacman frog's body language. If the Pacman frog is sticking to a corner, is making noises, has a bent or arched back and has his fur standing, then the Pacman frog is definitely upset and needs time to calm down.

13. Nipping

Pacman frogs have a tendency to nip. You should know that this is absolutely normal for a Pacman frog and that you can slowly train the Pacman frog not to exhibit such behavior. It is important that you understand the reason behind a Pacman frog's nipping. You should not harm the pet when he nips. This could scare him and will make things worse for you.

More often than not, Pacman frogs do so when they are in a playful mood. If your Pacman frog wants you to play with him, he could just signal you to do so by nipping. Such behavior is quite common in younger Pacman frogs, so don't be surprised when the young Pacman frog nips really hard.

Nipping comes very naturally to Pacman frogs. In their natural environment, Pacman frogs are known to nip each other, yet this does not harm them because of the quality of their skin. If you notice the skin of your pet, you will find it to be very thick. This thick skin is a cushion for the Pacman frog.

Another reason behind a Pacman frog's nipping is that the animal could be scared. When you bring the pet to your home for the first time, everything around him will be new. It is quite natural for the pet to get scared. This is the reason that nipping is very common in a new pet Pacman frog.

14. Sneezing

Another trait that will catch your eye very soon is the frequent sneezing of your Pacman frog. A Pacman frog is not very tall. His nose is very close to the ground, and on top of that the Pacman frog has a habit of smelling everything. This can cause dust to enter their nose, hence the sneezing.

While sneezing is normal for a Pacman frog, if you notice a runny nose, then you should definitely consult a veterinarian. This could mean that the Pacman frog has cold, and if not treated on time, it can get very serious.

Pacman frogs have a tendency to catch bacteria and viruses very easily. Therefore, you need to be on the lookout for the various symptoms. If the cold of the Pacman frog does not get better, he could get mucus and coughing, which can be very a serious problem. You should never compromise on the health of the pet.

15. Scratching

You will also catch your Pacman frog scratching itself multiple times. As a new owner, this could bug you, but you should know that this is very normal behavior. The skin of the Pacman frog is such that it can get itchy and the pet might have to scratch.

Though scratching is normal and nothing worrisome, if there are other symptoms that accompany it, then you need to see a vet. If the skin is red and shows abrasions, then this could be some allergy. You need to check with the vet to understand the condition.

The animal also has a tendency to catch fleas. If you spot fleas on the animal, don't ignore it. You can make use of anti-flea products for the pet and should consult the veterinarian if the symptoms persist.

16. Scooting

There may be times when you will spot your Pacman frog trying everything he can to move an object, even if it is too big for him. This will look particularly entertaining to many people as the Pacman frog tries very hard, but it the end gets nowhere. Don't worry, as this is just one of the games of the Pacman frog.

The pet will hold on to the object and will get as close to the object as possible. He will then scoot backwards and will try to drag the object. He might even start running in a circle. Your pet is an endearing animal, and he will always be up to some mischief or another.

17. Hiding objects

You might also find your Pacman frog hiding certain things. The thing with the Pacman frog is that they can get obsessed with certain things. For example, if there are ten toys in the Pacman frog's cage, he might get too attached to a couple of them. If he gets obsessed with something, he will not chew on it or harm it but will look for places to hide that thing.

Another thing with these pets is that they will not like you or anybody getting close to that object. For example, if you find out the hiding place of the Pacman frog's favorite toy and take it out from there, he will get very angry and stressed. So, you should definitely avoid giving your pet this kind of stress.

Your job should be to make sure that they are hiding stuff that is safe for him and not too relevant for you. You can't allow the pet to hide a knife or cupboard keys. Make sure you don't let them get obsessed with such things. Break the obsession right from the beginning, so that the pet can look for a new thing to get obsessed with and hide.

18. Wagging the tail

Another trait that you can expect from your Pacman frog is the wagging of the tail. This is a very lovable feature. Like most animals, the Pacman frog will wag its tail out of excitement. You can notice this behavior in Pacman frogs when they get along well with each other and when they are playing with each other.

Chapter 4: Setting up the Pacman frog's home

Like you need a home, an animal also needs a place and space that he can call his home. A home should make him happy and should be inviting for him. When the home does not provide the comfort and security that it should, it can lead to detrimental results.

There are many owners who might feel that there is no need to set up a cage because the pet can stay indoors. But, you need to remember that even if you are a hands-on parent, there will be times when the pet will be unsupervised.

There will be times when you will have to concentrate on some other work and the Pacman frog would be alone. The cage is very handy at such times because you can do your work and can also be sure that your pet is safe and sound in the cage that you have built for him.

Furthermore, during the nighttime, it is best for the pet and also for the family members that the pet sleeps in his cage. The pet will get used to the cage and your family members can also sleep without any tension of your pet being loose in the house.

When you are setting up a cage for the Pacman frog, you need to make sure that the cage is set up in a way that is inviting for the Pacman frog. The Pacman frog should not feel like a captive or a prisoner in the cage. If the frog is not comfortable, he will begin to get stressed, which is something that you wouldn't want.

The cage should be built keeping in mind the basic nature of the Pacman frog. You can't build a cage that is suitable for a tiger or a bird. You have a Pacman frog and your cage should be built keeping in mind his natural behavior, instincts, likes and dislikes. This is the best for you and also for the Pacman frog.

You should understand that just because the Pacman frog is a small animal does not mean that you can keep it anywhere. You need a proper cage for him. You should never keep him in a glass environment such as an aquarium. Such places don't allow the flow of air and can cause breathing issues in the Pacman frog.

It is important to have the right temperature for the Pacman frog. If the temperature is more than eighty degrees Fahrenheit or less than forty-five degree Fahrenheit, it is advised to keep the pet inside the house in controlled temperatures. Nothing is more important than the health and well being of the pet.

When you look for a cage for the Pacman frog, you will realize that there are great options available for cages in Pacman frog shops. You can buy a cage for as low as seventy-five dollars and also as high as one thousand dollars. It clearly depends on your choice and your budget.

1. Building the right cage

If you are looking at the measurements of the cage, then a cage of two feet high and three feet wide is suitable for a Pacman frog. This kind of a cage is suitable for up to three Pacman frogs. The type of cage you have will directly affect the physical health and mental health of your pet Pacman frog.

When you are building a cage for the Pacman frog, you have to make sure that you have provisions for the most basic and important things, such as food and water. The ideal cage will be spacious enough. It will allow the animal to roam around freely and rest well when it wants to.

You can use two big containers for food and water. It is important that the pet has access to food and water at all times. You don't want to be busy somewhere else when your pet is stressed with the lack of water.

While you make sure that food and water are available to the pet, you also have to make sure that the containers are not movable. The Pacman frog, owing to his natural tendency, might just kick the containers without realizing that the food and water in them was important for him.

To make things easier for you and the Pacman frog, you can attach the food and water containers to the cage. You will easily get the tools to do so. When you attach the containers, the Pacman frog can't move them. This will also help you to keep the cage clean and mess free.

The bedding that you choose for the Pacman frog should be comfortable. It should not occupy the entire cage because your pet needs some space to roam around also. You can get the right bedding for your pet Pacman frog from a pet store that sells Pacman frog products.

The best buy for a cage is one that can be cleaned easily. The cage should be comfortable and fun for the pet, but also easy to clean for you. You can go for a cage that has a bottom made of plastic and also coated wire. Such bottoms can be lifted for cleaning purposes.

Make sure that the wire can't be chewed. You can also go for a metal-bottomed cage, but you need to be extra careful with these kinds of cages. You will have to make sure that such cages are not exposed to feces and urine, otherwise they will rust. You can buy mats and rugs that can be thrown away after use to cover such bottoms.

A very important tip that you should always remember is that the cage bottom should not be covered with pine chips or cedar chips. These chips have certain oils that can cause damage to the liver of the animal and can also affect his respiratory system.

You might have seen Pacman frogs on display in a cage with pine chips or a glass aquarium with the chips, but if you wish to keep your Pacman frogs healthy, both the glass boxes and pine chips should be avoided. The simplest cage that you can build for your pet is a cage with fixed food and water containers and mats over wire mesh flooring.

You should also keep the litter box and the food and water containers on opposite sides. The Pacman frog would not want to defecate at a place where he eats food. You should also try to keep a hanging bottle of water along with the water bowl. This hanging bottle can be hung to the cage door.

You will have to take certain precautions with the litter box. The pet will try to dig in a very clean litter box. To avoid this issue, you should be keeping paper litter in the box. You can easily get paper litter that is recyclable. In addition, make sure that this is shredded or in pellets form.

If you get the clumping or the clay litter, these can get stuck in the nasal passage of the Pacman frog when they try to smell the box. While getting the cage done, you should remember that certain amount of privacy is needed by the pet Pacman frog.

If the Pacman frog does not get what it wants, the pet will get stressed and might withdraw from you. There should be darkness in the cage when the Pacman frog is fast asleep. You can even cover the top of the cage with a sheet or a blanket to make it really dark and secure for the pet Pacman frog.

It is important that the bedding of the pet is soft and comfortable so that he can slide in and feel comfortable. However, make sure that you check the bedding every day to know whether the pet Pacman frog has been chewing on its material. This can be dangerous, so you need to replace such items.

2. Accessories

Besides the basic stuff such as food and water, it is also important to accessorize the cage well. This is important because the right accessories will help him to feel like he is at home. They will bring him closer to his natural habitat and natural tendencies.

When you are looking to place the bedding in the cage, you should remember that the Pacman frog has a natural tendency to create and form burrows. He would want something that will help him emulate the action of digging. There are several accessories available these days that will help you to keep your Pacman frog happy.

A simple way to keep the Pacman frog happy is to give him an old t-shirt or piece of cloth. The Pacman frog will love it. He will act as if he is digging in the t-shirt. He will also try to fit in the t-shirt. This will keep him busy and happy. While the Pacman frog enjoys with the old cloth, you can bask in the happiness of your beloved pet.

If you go to a Pacman frog toyshop, you will get many ideas for the accessories that you can keep in the cage. There are many types of bedding available these days that can help your Pacman frog to have rest and also fun when he wants. For example, you can get bedding in the shape of a cave. This will be fun for the pet Pacman frog.

It is important that the toys are of a good quality. They should not be harmful for the pet, as he will take them in his mouth.

It is better if the toys are washable. This will enable you to wash the Pacman frog's toys every now and then when they are dirty. The harmful bacteria will also be removed from the toys when they are washed.

Furthermore, make sure that the toys can't be shredded by the Pacman frog. If the pet is able to shred the toy, he will swallow the shreds. This is very harmful and will only invite more trouble for the pet. To avoid all these issues, buy the right kind of toys.

If you are planning on domesticating more than one Pacman frog, you can consider buying another cage. This cage could be very simple and basic. The main purpose of this extra cage is to use it when one of the Pacman frogs is sick for isolation purposes.

A vet will always advise you to isolate a sick pet. This is necessary so that the pet can recuperate nicely in absence of other pets. He would need some space to himself. What is also important is that he should not transmit the disease to the healthy pets. The isolation helps to avoid such a situation also.

3. Cleaning the cage

Like it is important to clean the house that you dwell in, it is extremely important to clean the cage of the pet. You will not necessarily enjoy this process, but still you have to do it. The pet can't clean the cage on its own, and if it is forced to stay in an unhygienic environment, he will fall sick.

There are certain tasks that you need to do daily, while several others need to be done once a week. If the bedding is soiled, it should be cleaned on a daily basis. Similarly, if the food and water containers look dirty, they should be cleaned and refilled. The litter box needs to be cleared every day.

Once a week, you should clean the entire cage. You should thoroughly clean it with a clean cloth. Remember that the Pacman frog should not be in the cage when the cleaning procedure is going on. The litter box needs to be disinfected once a week. The toys of the Pacman frog should be washed once every two weeks, if the toys are washable.

The litter box and the floor of the cage can be cleaned with the help of a mixture of bleach and water. The mixture should have 98 per cent water and only two per cent bleach. This daily and weekly cleaning procedure is important so that the surroundings of the Pacman frog remain healthy. The bacteria in the dust and dirt can harm the Pacman frog.

While you are busy cleaning the cage of the pet Pacman frog, it is important that you check the cage thoroughly. If the Pacman frog has littered in an area other than the litter box, then it should be cleared and disinfected properly. You should make it a point to do this check on a daily basis.

You can keep baby wipes handy to clean something immediately. It is important that the cage is free from all bacteria and viruses that are known to cause diseases in pet animals. You should keep some time designated for the cleaning of the cage.

If you are using bleach to clean the litter box, then you should make sure that there is no residue on the box. The Pacman frog can try to lick any residue that he may find on the box or the cage. Bleach can be very harmful and dangerous to the pet animal.

Another point that you need to understand is that you should not use very strong disinfectants. Such products can be very harmful if they ingested even in the smallest of quantities. You should always look for mild anti-bacterial soaps and detergents to clean the vessels and the floor.

A simple procedure that you can follow once a week to clean the cage thoroughly is to fill a bucket with clean water. Pour some anti-bacterial detergent that you wish to use. Form a nice lather in the bucket. This can be used to clean the toys and the containers. The remaining can be used to clean the floor.

After you have cleaned the floor with the detergent, use plain water to wash off any sign of the detergent. This will ensure that the Pacman frog does not ingest anything harmful.

It is also very important that you let the floor dry completely before you allow the Pacman frog to come inside the cage. He could spoil the floor and could create a mess for you to clean again. He could even try to drink any residue that he finds on the floor. To avoid all these hassles, you should allow the floor to dry completely.

Chapter 5: Frog-proofing the house

When you have a Pacman frog at home, you have to ensure that the pet is safe at all times. The Pacman frog is so tiny that you might not know where he is most of the time. This makes it very important that you understand the behavior of your pet very well.

A Pacman frog has a very curious personality. He will not think twice before charging into unknown territory. You might be busy with some work, and before you know your pet Pacman frog might be walking into some real danger.

You should know that a Pacman frog has a tendency to injure himself. If you don't pay attention, the damage could be very serious and irrevocable.

A solution to keep your Pacman frog safe is to proof your home. This chapter will discuss the potential dangers to the Pacman frogs and also some simple ways to Pacman frog proof your house.

1. How to frog proof the house

This section will help you to understand the various ways to Pacman frog proof your home. Make sure you Pacman frog proof your home and keep your pet Pacman frog away from potential dangers.

There is no use to cry after the damage has been done. It is always better to take the necessary precautions in the very beginning.

To begin with, you should make sure that all liquid chemicals are far away from the Pacman frog. If a chemical is in reach of the Pacman frog, he might accidently spill it all over him.

To make sure that nothing of the sort happens, you should make sure that all such supplies are kept in top cabinets where a Pacman frog can't reach.

You should also make sure that all kind of medicines, syrups and tablets are out of the reach of the Pacman frog. These can be very harmful for the pet. You can also get childproof cabinets in your home to keep all such potentially dangerous things in those cabinets.

You would be surprised to know that your pet can climb toilets. Just imagine what can happen if the seat is not kept down. The Pacman frog can slip inside and can get himself killed. To avert any such incident, make sure that the toilet seat is kept down. This should be done especially when the Pacman frog is around the toilet area.

You can also keep the toilet door closed to make sure that he does not enter the toilet. If there are any areas of the house that the Pacman frog needs to keep away from, you have to keep them closed and blocked. If you don't do so, the pet can just enter the space when you are not around.

You should make sure that the Pacman frog sleeps in his cage. This is for his safety and also for the good of the family members. You can also keep him in the cage when you can't supervise him.

You should make sure that your Pacman frog plays with the right kind of toys. Cheap plastic materials that can have an adverse effect on the health of the Pacman frog must be avoided. Similarly, toys that can be shredded or broken should also be avoided.

Your Pacman frog will shock you with the kind of things it can get hurt from. For example, the cardboard rolls of toilet paper can be very harmful for the Pacman frog because he can get his head stuck in it.

You should make sure any such potentially dangerous things are out of the reach of the Pacman frog. Keep the waste bin and waste stuff away from him because he might try to play with things that could be harmful for him.

This might be very difficult for you in the beginning to look into areas and places that have hidden dangers for the pet, but you will definitely learn with time and experience. The furniture in the house should be Pacman frog-friendly. You should make sure there are no sharp edges that could hurt the animal

If you have recliners in your house, keep them away from the pet. The pet could be severely injured by these reclining chairs. If somebody sits on them accidentally while the Pacman frog is hiding in the spring, the reclining action and the spring could injure the pet. To be on the safer side, always check the chair or sofa that you are about to sit on.

Your Pacman frog could climb onto the washing machine and dishwasher, so make sure that these items always have a lid on. To be on the safer side, always check inside the washing machine and the dishwasher before operating them.

The pet Pacman frog should stay away from the plants of the house. You should also make sure that he stays away from Styrofoam products. All kinds of sponges should not be in the reach of the Pacman frog. The Pacman frog could bite into them and swallow them. This can be potentially very dangerous.

Rubber items can also be very dangerous if they are swallowed by the pet Pacman frog. Imagine the kind of damage a rubber band can do if the Pacman frog swallows it. You should know that the Pacman frog will not know what he is not supposed to do. You will have to keep him away from danger. This includes both soft rubber and foam rubber products. You should also make sure that soaps and detergents are kept away from the reach of the pet. These items can be very dangerous for the pet. The Pacman frog could even up counters and reach such things.

It is better to use the cabinets of bathrooms and rooms to keep things away from the pet Pacman frog. You should make sure that the pet stays away from stacks of clothes. Keep the cupboards locked and keep the laundry area closed and locked. If the Pacman frog gets inside a stack of clothes, you will have a very hard time finding him.

There could be so many things in your house that look non-dangerous, but could be very dangerous for your Pacman frog. This is the reason that you might have to monitor the pet animal when he is not in his cage.

It is also a good idea to designate a spare room in the house for the Pacman frog. This room should be open and spacious. It should have natural light and dim artificial lights.

You can leave the Pacman frog in the room and be sure that he is playing and having a good time. Of course, this will totally depend on whether you can spare a room in the house or not.

2. Areas of hidden dangers

It is very important to look for areas of hidden dangers and keep the pet safe. The Pacman frog will try to chew anything it can.

You should be on the lookout of any telltale signs. If you see stuffing material on the floor, you should know what the Pacman frog has been up to. He should be stopped as soon as possible.

Keep away your shoes in a cupboard or cabinet. Before you know, your Pacman frog might start hiding in them and chewing on them. You should also check the bedding of the pet on a regular basis.

If he has been chewing on it, then you should try a better and stronger fabric. These things are very harmful for the Pacman frog.

Pacman frogs are also attracted to plants. They will merrily chew on the leaves of various plants. Many plants are known to be poisonous for the Pacman frog, so they should not be encouraged to eat the leaves.

The best thing to do will obviously be to keep the plants in an area where the Pacman frog can't reach them. This is a foolproof way to keep them away from the plants.

If you observe the pet closely, you will start understanding his likes and preferences. After you have kept an eye on him for a few days, you will start understanding his favorite spots in the house.

You will know which areas he likes to dig and where he prefers to hide. These pieces of information can help you to Pacman frog proof your home in a better way.

The Pacman frog will go to a recently cleaned bathtub or toilet and lick the water off the surface. While this could be fun to watch for you, it could be dangerous if the tub and toilet still have traces of the detergent.

To be on the safer side, you should always rinse the surfaces with excess water. This will make sure that the detergent has been washed off.

A Pacman frog has a tendency to walk in to a situation and then not know what to do next. For example, a Pacman frog might get under the small opening of a fridge or refrigerator. This is very dangerous because the fan of the fridge can harm him.

You might also have to use barriers to make sure that the Pacman frog can't reach certain spots and rooms in the house. A point that needs to be noted here is that normal pet barriers can't be used for a Pacman frog.

Even child proofing barriers would not be effective. This is because your Pacman frog will happily climb these barriers. He might even get his head stuck in the barrier openings, inviting more trouble for himself and for you also.

You will have to make safe and secure barriers on your own. Or, you could get these barriers from a Pacman frog shop. These barriers have a very strong base of plastic.

Barriers made of Plexiglas will also serve the purpose right. If you wish to make the barrier at your home, then you can use Plexiglas or wood.

You can also use a good piece of cardboard as a barrier. For example, to keep the Pacman frog away from the fridge or refrigerator, you can fix the cardboard in the opening. This will prevent the pet from entering the opening. Make sure you use a good quality cardboard.

You can also take some measures to keep the Pacman frog away from your furniture. This is important so that they don't try to create a tunnel by chewing on the fabric. You can fix some heavy material of cardboard at the bottom end of the furniture that you are trying to protect.

This can prevent the pet from digging on the material of the furniture. You can also keep such barriers in front of various rooms. This will make sure that the pet can't enter these rooms. These are simple ways to keep the pet safe and also your things safe.

It is important that you take appropriate steps to Pacman frog proof the home. This will help you to set some limits and boundaries for the pet. These boundaries are for his own good.

There is no use in getting cautious after serious and irrevocable damage has been done. It pays to take all the necessary precautions right from the very beginning.

You will take some time to understand the mannerisms of your pet. It is important to always supervise the pet. If you are unable to do so, you can ask a family member to do so for you.

You can use the cage when there is no one around to supervise the pet Pacman frog.

You can be secure knowing that you pet is safe and sound inside its cage. But, once you understand the pet better, you can further steps to make sure that things remain safe in the house for the pet. A safe environment is good for everybody in the home.

Chapter 6: Dietary requirements

As the owner or as the prospective owner of a Pacman frog, it should be your foremost concern to provide adequate and proper nutrition to the pet. If the pet animal in deficient in any nutrient, he will develop various deficiencies and acquire many diseases. When the nutrition is right, you can easily ward off many dangerous diseases.

Each animal species is different. Just because certain kinds of foods are good for your pet dog, it does not mean that they will be good for your pet Pacman frog also.

It is important to learn about all the foods that the Pacman frogs are naturally inclined towards eating. You should always be looking at maintaining the good health of your pet.

It is important to learn about the foods that are good for your Pacman frog. However, you should also understand that the foods that you feed your pet could be lacking in certain nutrients.

An animal in the wild is different from one in captivity. The availability of certain foods will also affect the diet of your pet. If such is the case, you will have to give commercial pellets to your Pacman frog. These pellets are known to compensate for the various nutritional deficiencies that the animal might have due to malnutrition.

You should always aim at providing wholesome nutrition to your pet. It is important to understand the pet's nutritional requirements and include all the nutrients in his daily meals. To meet his nutritional requirements, you might also have to give him certain supplements.

The supplements will help you to make up for the essential nutrients that are not found in his daily meals.

Though these supplements are easily available, you should definitely consult a veterinarian before you give your Pacman frog any kind of supplements.

It is very important that you serve only high quality food to your pet. If you are trying to save some money by buying cheaper, low quality alternatives, then you are in a bad situation. Low quality food will affect the health of the Pacman frog.

You can expect him to acquire deficiencies and diseases when he is not fed good quality food. The cure for this is taking the pet to the veterinarian. This in turn will only cost you more money.

To avoid this endless loop, it is better to work on the basics. Keep the pet healthy by feeding him with high quality foods, rather than spending money on him by taking him to the veterinarian.

1. Nutritional needs

It is critical that you understand the specific nutritional needs of your pet Pacman frog. A Pacman frog that dwells freely in the wild is used to having a high protein diet. This protein basically comes from the carnivorous diet of the Pacman frog.

Pacman frogs love their meat. If you are planning on keeping your Pacman frog on a strict plant diet, then you are in for a big shock. These carnivorous animals need animal-based protein in their diet.

The food that you serve to the Pacman frog should have at least 35 per cent protein. It is better if the amount of protein is more than 35 per cent.

The food of a Pacman frog should also be rich in fats. The carnivorous diet of the Pacman frog in the wild provides it with all the necessary fats.

The fat content should be at least 20 per cent of the food. The protein and the fat in the diet of the Pacman frog are suited to the kind of digestive system that it has.

The digestive tract of a Pacman frog is quite small. This kind of digestive tract is suitable to digest good quality and easy to digest animal protein.

It is not very suitable for food items such as corn, grain, and large quantities of vegetables and fruits. The main component of your Pacman frog's main feed should be animal protein.

The Pacman frog also needs the nutrient taurine. This is utilized by the cardiovascular system of the Pacman frog and also the eyes. The food that you serve your pet should have sufficient quantities of taurine. This means that you should keep the pet away from dog food, because it is known to lack in this vital nutrient.

The Pacman frog needs more of animal protein for maintaining its bodily functions. The dog food is known to be rich in plant protein, but not animal protein.

Cecum is a part of the digestive system that helps the body to break down plant proteins. Pacman frogs don't have Cecum in their body.

2. Every day diet of Pacman frogs

If you are looking at buying food from the grocery store, then don't forget to check all the ingredients. If the main component is not meat, then you should leave the food item.

There will be many food items that will have cereal or corn or grain as the main ingredient. You should avoid such food items.

You should look for Pacman frog foods in the pet shop to get the best food for your pet. Cat food or kitten food will not be the best buy for your pet. These food items will be unable to provide the right kind of nutrition to the Pacman frog.

In case Pacman frog food is not available in your area and you are only left with the choice of kitten and cat food, then you should consult a veterinarian for the right cat food.

There are all sorts of cat foods available. You should buy the one that is the best for your Pacman frog. Even in this case, you have to use fatty acid supplements along with the food to make up for the lack of fatty acids in cat and kitten food.

It is always a good idea to consult a vet in case of any doubts that you might be having regarding the diet and foods of the Pacman frog.

One of the best food items that take care of the protein and the fat content required by the Pacman frog is 'Total Pacman frog'. It has over 35 per cent animal protein and over 20 per cent fat that are essential for the growth of the Pacman frog.

The main component of the Pacman frog's meal should be chicken. You can replace chicken with lamb if you wish to.

If you are looking for Pacman frog foods, then this should be the main ingredient of the food item. Don't forget to check the percentage of each nutrient in the food item.

Many a times, store bought foods are preserved by artificial means. You should not be buying such food products for your Pacman frog.

If the food item is preserved with the addition of Vitamin E in it, then this food is healthy for your Pacman frog. It is also important that the food item is not mixed with artificial colors.

As the parent of the pet Pacman frog, you will be required to make smart choices in order to provide wholesome nutrition to your pet.

Another thing that you need to make sure of while buying food for Pacman frog is that the food should not have vegetables and fruits in dry form. This is extremely unhealthy for the pet.

Dried forms of vegetables and fruits are easily available, so many manufacturers might decide to use them. But, they can cause a serious health hazard to your pet Pacman frog. They can get stuck in the digestive tract or intestine and can cause very harmful gastro intestinal issues. You should also avoid any food that has a high percentage of corn or grain or both.

You should make sure that your Pacman frog is getting optimal nutrition in his diet. His food should provide him with all the essential nutrients and vitamins.

A high quality Pacman frog food will help you to fulfill the daily nutritional requirements of the Pacman frog. These foods will contain animal protein and all other nutrients in the right quantity.

If Pacman frog food is not available, you might have to shift to cat or kitten food. But, this food would not be able to provide all the essential nutrients to your pet.

There will more fiber than required and less quantities of animal protein. If you don't supplement the diet of the Pacman frog, your Pacman frog will suffer from some serious health issues.

Over the period of time, the skin of the pet will start to dull. This is one of the first signs that something is not right with the pet's health.

The malnutrition will result in many other health issues. In severe cases, you can also expect kidney stones to be formed along with bladder stones. The reason for these stones is the excess fiber in the cat and kitten food.

If you have no other choice but to choose from cat and kitten food, then you should definitely go for kitten food.

The reason behind this choice is that kitten food has relatively higher percentage of protein when compared with equal quantities of cat food. Also, the fat content of kitten food is much higher than similar quantities of cat food.

It is also important to note that if a larger quantity of cat food is fed to the Pacman frog for a longer duration of time, then the Pacman frog can be diagnosed with insulinomas. This is the reason that you need to consult the vet before feeding the pet with any other food apart from Pacman frog food.

If you have been feeding the Pacman frog with the wrong kind of foods, you need to switch as soon as possible. No matter how much damage has been done, you can still avoid a lot of damage. So, never fail to make the right choices and right switches.

Your food choices will be limited by the area you live in, but there is always a way to make sure that the optimal thing is being done for the Pacman frog.

There are many people who feed their pet Pacman frog with cooked chicken along with standard kitten food. This makes sure that the Pacman frog gets optimal amounts of protein and fat.

If you are also looking to feed the pet Pacman frog with cooked chicken then you can look at serving the skin, heart, breast and liver. There are people who serve raw chicken to the Pacman frog along with the kitten food. The problem with raw chicken is that it can introduce many disease-causing parasites in the pet's intestine.

If you wish to save your Pacman frog from these parasites then the raw chicken should be frozen. This will kill most of the disease-causing parasites. Before you can serve the raw frozen chicken to the pet, it should be thawed properly.

Another simple way to enhance the nutritional value of the pet's food is by allowing the Pacman frog to chew and lick the softer ends of long chicken bones.

Letting the Pacman frog feed on the bone marrow has a lot of advantages. It is a natural source of many needed nutrients. The animal will get its required quantity of Calcium from the bone marrow. Calcium is required for some essential body functions.

Another alternative that you can consider to supplement the main meals of the pet Pacman frog is the easily available chicken baby food. You should make sure that this is only a supplement and not the regular meal. While you allow your pet to chew and the lick the bones, should make sure that the bones are of the right size.

If the bones are too small in size, the pet might just swallow the entire piece, leading to a detrimental blockage of the digestive tract. You should give bigger bones that can only be licked but not swallowed. In case you wish to feed the Pacman frog with the big bones, make sure you boil these before serving them to the pet. This will make the bones softer for the pet.

It is always better if you can feed the Pacman frog with high quality Pacman frog food and also raw meat with it. A diet like this will take care of the nutritional requirements of the pet. The pet should have access to water and also food at all times. You need not worry about the Pacman frog over eating. It is known that these animals don't overeat. They eat as much as is required by their body, but they need frequent meals, so it is better that they have easy access to food.

The pet would require almost 10 small meals a day, owing to the fast metabolism of the Pacman frog. The water can be kept in a container with a heavy base. In addition, keep some water in a water bottle that can hang from the cage. You should change the contents of the containers twice a day. You might have to do it more if the pet has soiled the food or water while playing.

You may have to make changes to the Pacman frog's diet as it grows older. It is known that older Pacman frogs can have kidney issues. To lower the pressure on the kidneys, you should give the pet a diet low in animal protein. There are special diets for older frogs, such as the 'totally Pacman frog for old Pacman frogs'. You could also switch to a diet plan to maintain older cats, but this should be done only if the Pacman frog is above four years of age and that too after consulting the veterinarian.

3. Introducing new foods and switching foods

When you get a kit home, one of the biggest concerns that you will have is regarding its diet. It will take some time to understand the dietary preferences of the new Pacman frog. Pacman frogs form their preferences quite early in their lives. It is said that in the first six months, the Pacman frog develops his food preferences.

This means that the first six months is a great time for you to introduce different kinds of foods to the Pacman frog. This will help him to have his preferences and will also make things easier for you. If your Pacman frog likes three kinds of food items instead of one, it gets easier for you also.

In case a certain food item is not available, you know that you have other choices. If you don't introduce new foods to the Pacman frog, he will turn out to be a very fussy and you, as the parent, will have a hard time keeping his taste buds happy.

If you want to introduce new foods or switch foods, you can't suddenly change his usual meal plan. This will put off the Pacman frog. There are some simple tips and tricks that you should be following to make sure that the pet is eating well even when new foods are being introduced.

A simple way of introducing new food in the diet of the Pacman frog is by starting out with a small amount of the food. Take a bowl and add the usual food of the pet in it. Now, take very small amount of the new food that you wish to feed your pet in the bowl. Mix the contents and serve the food to the Pacman frog.

You should know that your Pacman frog can outsmart you easily in this case. He will eat the usual food and might just leave the new food. This is because the new food item is alien to him. He needs time to get used to it, but there is nothing to worry about even if the pet leaves the new food in the beginning.

Just keep adding a very small amount of the food item in the usual food of the pet. Initially, the Pacman frog will get used to the smell of the new food. This might take some time, so be prepared to it. Once you see that the pet Pacman frog has started eating the new food along with the usual old food, you can gradually increase the portion of the new food and decrease the portion of the old usual food.

Another trick to get the Pacman frog accustomed to the smell of the new food item is by keeping the old and new food together. For example, you can store the two foods together in a container or in a zip lock. When you do this, the smells will get intermingled. So, now even when you serve the pet with the usual food, you are serving him the smell of the new one.

The given process will take some days, but you will have to have some patience. The idea is to help the Pacman frog get used to the scent of a food before you can expect the pet to eat the food. Once he is okay with the scent, he will try out the food item on his own.

If you are looking for another trick to introduce new food items and switch between food items, then there is another one for you. Take some water in a bowl and add the two food items in the bowl. You can keep the quantity of the old food item a little more than the new one. Now, just stir this mixture and heat it for some time.

Don't heat the mixture of the food items for too long. You just need to heat it for seconds so that the smells blend with one another. If you still have your doubts whether your pet Pacman frog will eat the food or not, then you can add 5-7 drops of 'Pacman frogone' in the bowl. This 'Pacman frogone' or kibble gravy is loved by Pacman frogs.

When you serve this food mix to the Pacman frog, it is like a treat for him. He will waste no time in eating and licking the kibble gravy. In the process, he will also eat the contents of the bowl. This is a simple trick to make your pet eat new foods. This trick is also useful when the Pacman frog is sick and is refusing to eat anything.

A point that should be noted here is that you should throw away the contents of the bowl that your pet does not eat. Don't keep it to serve him in the next meal. This is because the kibble gravy and water will cause the food items to spoil if they are kept for too long.

Treats

Treats are an essential part of a pet's meal plan. Treats are like small meal gifts that make the pet happy and delighted. The anticipation of getting a treat can also keep his behavior in check. You should work on giving your pet high quality treats. This section will give you an idea of the kind of treats you can include in your Pacman frog's meal plan.

It should be noted that just because your Pacman frog seems to enjoy a treat, you can't give the food item to him all day long. You will have to keep a check on the amount of treats a Pacman frog will get. This is important because treats are not food replacements. They are only small rewards.

It is also important that the pet Pacman frog associates the treat with rewards. He should know that he is being served the treat reward for a reason. You should also make sure that the treats are healthy for the pet. If you keep serving him the wrong kinds of treats, it will only affect his health in the long run. This is the last thing that you would want as a parent of the pet.

This section will help you understand various kinds of treats that you can serve your pet. The best kind of treat for a Pacman frog is a food item that has meat as its main component. Pacman frogs love their meat, and it is also healthy for them.

You should always look for treats that are healthy for the pet. The pet should enjoy eating them, but their nutrition should not be compromised. What is the fun of a treat if it is followed by multiple veterinarian visits? Your main aim should be to satisfy the pet's taste buds and also provide him with some nutrition.

You should also make an attempt to understand what is there in the treat that you prefer for the Pacman frog. If you know the contents and their exact quantities, it will only get easier for you to make a well-informed decision. Various pet shops will have Pacman frog foods that will help you to make a decision regarding the pet's treats.

The treat should have the right mix of vitamins, fatty acids, minerals and proteins This will make the treat healthy and wholesome. It is better if the treat has no sugar contents. This is because the sugar will add no food value to the treat. Such healthy treats can be given to the pet Pacman frog on a daily basis without any issues.

Be careful if you are planning on giving your pet a bowl of fruits as a treat. If you think that a fruit or vegetable can serve as a treat for the pet, then you are absolutely wrong. The small intestines of the animal are not well equipped to digest such things. Though a small amount of these foods should be fine, a larger quantity will affect the health of the pet.

The pet can suffer from diarrhea and other gastrointestinal problems because of consuming large amount of fruits and vegetables. You will be shocked to know the problems that an undigested vegetable or fruit can cause in a Pacman frog. If there is a piece of undigested fruit or vegetable in the digestive tract of the animal, it can lead to obstructions and blockages.

The bowel movements of the pet can be restricted or completely stopped because of the undigested food. This can even pose a very serious threat to the life of the animal.

You should limit the consumption of fruits and vegetables to once or twice a week for the Pacman frog. Even when you decide to give him these foods, remember to keep the quantity very low.

Furthermore, you should make sure that you peel and mash the items before you serve them to the animal. This will allow him to digest the food well. There have been many reports of blockages in Pacman frogs because of undigested carrots.

The Pacman frog needs to get its daily dose of meat, so you should include in some quantity in the treat also. Give 3-4 drops of Pacman frogone as a part of the treat. Your pet will love it.

You can also give him a small piece of Pacman frogvite. Remember to keep the quantity very low because this can increase the sugar content in the pet's body and can also lead to toxicity.

You should keep in mind that you shouldn't serve something as a treat to the pet just because you like the food item. The food item should not harm the very sensitive digestive tract of the Pacman frog.

As a rule, stay away from sodas, dairy products that are not for lactose intolerants, candy bars, chocolate pieces, caffeine, nuts and excessively salty and sugary foods.

These food items can cause some serious damage to the Pacman frog. For example, if a nut gets stuck in the digestive tract, it can eve kill the Pacman frog. Excessive amount of sugar can directly affect the work of the pancreas and the blood sugar level in the body.

Dairy products are known to cause gastrointestinal issues in these animals. Also, a large amount of salt is unhealthy for the Pacman frog. He can get really sick if you feed him with foods such as chips.

Look for Pacman frog foods or kitten foods that can be served as treats. For example, Eukanuba Kitten food is a great example of nutritious yet tasty treat for the Pacman frog. Another example of a great treat is the Gerber chicken baby food.

Give your pet different kinds of Pacman frog foods so that you get a lot of options to choose from. You can also buy small chew toys from him from the Pacman frog store. The Pacman frog will love this. You can also give him shreds of chicken or small pieces of boiled eggs as a treat.

4. Supplements

The diet of the Pacman frog should be highly nutritious. If you make sure that the Pacman frog is getting all its necessary nutrients from the food itself, you can avoid the use of supplements. At times, your Pacman frog's diet might not be able to provide it with the right set of nutrients and vitamins. In such a case, it becomes necessary to introduce supplements in the diet of the Pacman frog.

If the pet is not well and is recovering from an injury or disease, the veterinarian might advise you to administer certain supplements to the pet. These supplements will help the pet to heal faster and get back on his feet sooner.

You should always consult a veterinarian before you administer any supplement to the Pacman frog. He will be the best judge of which supplements the Pacman frog requires and which ones he doesn't.

There are many vitamin supplements that are available in tasty treat forms for the Pacman frog. While you can be sure that your pet is getting the right nutrients, the pet can enjoy the treat given to him.

You can also include supplements of fatty acids in the diet of the Pacman frog. A few drops of this kind of supplement will enhance the taste and the nutritional value of the food item that is being served to the Pacman frog.

While it can be necessary to supplement certain vitamins and nutrients to the pet, you should also be aware of the hazards of over feeding a certain nutrient. If there is an overdose of a certain vitamin in the body of the Pacman frog, it can lead to vitamin toxicity.

Vitamin A toxicity is very common in Pacman frogs. You should try to feed the Pacman frog with an optimal amount of Vitamin A to avoid such a condition. You might even see that your pet is enjoying all the supplements, but this in no way means that you can give him an overdose. You should always do what is right for the Pacman frog's health.

Another point that you should take care of is that you should not blindly follow the instructions and dosage that is printed on various supplements. The food that you feed the Pacman frog will also have a supply of vitamins. The Pacman frog will only require some extra dosage.

On a regular basis, you can look at giving the Pacman frog treats with supplements, such as Pacman frogone and Pacman frogvite. These can be given on a daily basis, but the portions need to be controlled.

You can five 3-6 drops of Pacman frogone and pea-sized portion of Pacman frogvite. This is enough to supplement the daily requirements of the Pacman frog.

Chapter 7: The health of the Pacman frog

An unhealthy pet can be a nightmare for any owner. The last thing that you would want is to see your pet in pain. Many disease-causing parasites dwell in unhygienic places and food. If you take care of the hygiene and food of the Pacman frog, there are many diseases that you can avoid.

At times, even after all the precautions that you take, the pet can get sick. It is always better to be well equipped so that you can help your pet. You should always consult a vet when you find any unusual traits and symptoms in the pet.

You should understand the various health-related issues that your pet Pacman frog can suffer from. This knowledge will help you to get the right treatment at the right time. It is also important that you understand how you can take care of a sick pet. This knowledge will help you to keep your calm and help the sick Pacman frog.

1. Common health issues

Pacman frogs are prone to certain diseases such as adrenal diseases. You should know that the unique digestive system, fast metabolism and smaller size can cause the pet to get sick very easily. If proper care is not taken, you will find your pet getting sick very often.

This section will help you to understand the various diseases that a Pacman frog can suffer from. The various symptoms and causes are also discussed in detail. This will help you to recognize a symptom, which would have otherwise gone unnoticed.

Though the section helps you to understand the various common health problems of the Pacman frog, it should be understood that a vet should be consulted in case of any health related issue. A vet will physically examine the pet and suggest what is best for your pet Pacman frog.

The various diseases that your Pacman frog can suffer from are as follows:

Adrenal disease
Adrenal disease occurs when the adrenal gland in the body malfunctions. A Pacman frog is prone to this disease. The main cause is the growth of cells on a gland called the adrenal gland. This growth can be present on the left or the right adrenal gland.

The growth on the gland can be both benign and cancerous. Though both the adrenal glands can possess such a growth, but it is said that the left gland is more prone to this disease than the right one.

It is generally noticed that Pacman frogs at the age of 3-4 years suffer from this disease, but in many cases Pacman frogs below the age of three have also known to suffer from the adrenal disease.

Though the disease is very common in Pacman frogs, this disease can be difficult to diagnose. One of the major effects of adrenal disease is a change in the hormonal production of the Pacman frog. This can often mislead many people. A drastic change in hormonal characteristics and production is often associated with Cushing's disease, however this disease does not affect Pacman frogs.

Another problem with the diagnosis of the adrenal disorder is that the blood reports will be normal for the Pacman frog, indicating that all is fine with the animal. Even the X-ray reports will not show any issue.

There are however some special blood tests that can be done for the Pacman frogs to diagnose the adrenal disorder. You should make sure that your veterinarian has the facility to consult these specialized blood tests.

It is important to understand that there are still many places and hospitals that don't have the facility to conduct these blood tests. In these cases, you will have to depend on the diagnosis of your veterinarian.

It is important that your veterinarian has the expertise to treat Pacman frogs. This will help him to read the symptoms correctly.

The exact cause of this disease is still not known. Though various tests are being done, the exact cause of adrenal disease still remains to be known. According to one theory, the spaying and neutering of Pacman frogs before they are sexually mature can lead to this condition.

There is another theory, according to which the exposure to too much artificial light can lead to this health condition in Pacman frogs. A Pacman frog is not very comfortable in extremely hot or cold temperatures. This is the reason that most owners keep their pet Pacman frog indoors.

Keeping the Pacman frog inside a room with artificial sources of light disrupts the natural cycle of the pet to a great extent. The artificial lights can lead to this malfunctioning of the adrenal gland. Another reason behind this condition is high stress levels in Pacman frogs.

You should try to keep your Pacman frog away from too much exposure to artificial lights. It is not possible to completely break the natural cycle of the pet, but there are a few precautions that you can. The cage of the Pacman frog should have no source of artificial light.

In the evening time or when the weather is pleasant, you should take the pet out in the open. Allow him to play in a safe area. This will expose him to some natural light. When he is indoors, you can make sure that he is exposed to dull lights.

You should not keep the Pacman frog in the dark and stress him out, just try to expose him to dull lights rather than exposing him to very bright artificial lights. The room should be exposed to the natural light cycles. It should not be artificially lit all the time.

If your kit is not spayed or neutered when you buy or adopt him, you should remember not to do it until the Pacman frog is at least four to six months of age. A Pacman frog will attain adulthood by six months, so it is better to wait till then.

You should also try to keep the stress levels of the Pacman frog to a bare minimum. Don't put him in the cage at all times. Let him be in a Pacman frog proof room of the house and also allow him to play in the open spaces of the house.

Symptoms:

Because the diagnosis of this disorder can be difficult, it makes it all the more important to read the symptoms well. You can look out for the following symptoms in the Pacman frog to know that he is suffering from this particular disease:

- You will notice sudden and drastic weight loss in the pet.
-
- The skin of the Pacman frog can get very flaky. You will also notice that the skin appears itchy and it will develop sores with time.
-
- Males and females can show some unique symptoms also. For example, you might notice that the male is very active during mating and otherwise he shows lethargy in his movements and actions.
-
- The female Pacman frog will also show certain symptoms that can help you to diagnose this health condition. For example, the vulva of

the female will be swollen because of the growth on the adrenal glands.

Treatment:

In some cases, the animal is kept on a strict dose of certain medication. However, it should be noted here that this is not the permanent cure for adrenal disease.

If you wish to cure the pet fully, the affected part of the adrenal gland will have to be removed from the animal's body. Then they must take medication have to help the other part of the gland to recover and function properly.

The disease and its treatment can have complications depending on the kind of tumor and also on the location of the tumor. If the outgrowth is cancerous, it automatically complicates the surgery. A metastasized tumor presents difficulties of removal, which complicates the process.

If the affected adrenal gland is the left one, the surgery is relatively simpler than when the right one is affected. The surgery on the right gland poses a danger to the major vena cava because the two are close together.

There is a danger of rupturing the vein. If the entire right gland is not operated on, then the symptoms can return.

Insulinomas

Low blood sugar in Pacman frogs leads to a condition called Insulinomas. When the Pacman frog develops a condition in which he has an abnormal growth over his pancreas that releases insulin, it is referred to as Insulinomas.

The release of this insulin in the blood stream leads to a condition of low blood pressure or hypoglycemia in the animal.

It is also important to note that these growths could either be cancerous or non-cancerous in nature. If the condition is not treated, it can get very serious and can even lead to the animal's death. A Pacman frog over the age of three is susceptible to this disease.

You should be on the lookout for the energy levels of the Pacman frog. If he sleeps more than his usual sleeping hours and is lethargic, you should know that something is wrong. Talk to his veterinarian and get his blood test done.

The exact cause of this health condition is still not known, but in most cases it has been noticed that this disease either accompanies or follows the adrenal disease.

Because this disease is related to the pancreas, this condition is definitely affected by the kind of simple carbohydrates the pet is fed.

The high amount of sugar in the diet of the Pacman frog could also be a precursor to the disease. It is often advised that a Pacman frog be served a protein rich diet.

You should limit the carbohydrates and sugar and increase the amount of proteins in the pet's diet. Even the treats that are served to the pet Pacman frog should be healthy and not just sugar candies.

If you don't provide adequate amounts of protein in the diet of the animal, you will see him suffering from many ailments. There is no proof that a high protein diet can help you to avoid this condition, but it will definitely help in the Pacman frog's growth and development.

Symptoms:

You can look out for the following symptoms in the Pacman frog to know that he is suffering from this particular disease:

- You will notice the Pacman frog to be very lazy and lethargic. It will appear that he has no energy to do anything.
-
- He will sleep a lot. If you try to wake him up, he can be unresponsive.
-
- Your pet will experience disorientation. He will not feel or seem coordinated in his actions or movements.
-
- The Pacman frog will drool and might also vomit occasionally. The pet will lose his appetite and will not show any interest in eating his food. He might also detest his favorite foods.
-
- Another symptom that can help you understand that your pet is suffering from Insulinomas is that he will experience seizures. You will notice sudden and jerky movements in the limbs of the pet. This could be accompanied by sudden passage of urine. He can also make sounds while he is sleeping.

Treatment:

One of the first things that you need to do when you see the pet suffering from a seizure is to apply Karo syrup over his gums. This syrup will help the pet to come out of a seizure that is related to hypoglycemia.

But, the application of the Karo syrup is by no means a permanent fix to the Pacman frog's problem. This is only a temporary relief to the poor pet.

Even after the temporary relief, you can expect another seizure very soon. This is because of the increased production of insulin in the Pacman frog. You should visit the veterinarian as soon as possible to get the Pacman frog tested. The vet will also give medication of Prednisolone to make sure that the blood sugar is stabilized.

He or she might also suggest surgery to operate on the growth on the pancreas. But, a major problem is that Insulinomas can reoccur. There is no permanent cure for this health condition.

Another complication that can arise from Insulinomas is that it can spread from the pancreas to other organs. This can be very detrimental to the Pacman frog's health.

In most cases, the vet advises surgery and continued medication for the pet. You would also have to ensure that you feed the pet with high protein and low carbohydrates in his meals.

ECE

Epizootic catarrhal enteritis is a virus that is known to attack Pacman frogs. The intestine of the animal is affected by this virus. It causes a disease that is called the Green slime disease. While you might think that a case of diarrhea is not very serious, you need to watch out.

This virus can cause malnutrition and dehydration in the pet, which can take the shape of ulcers. A Pacman frog that is old in age will be at the risk of ECE, but this does not mean that a kit can't be attacked by ECE.

The symptoms in a kit are usually very subdued. If the Pacman frog is already suffering from an illness, he is likely to be going through this also.

Symptoms:

-   One of the first symptoms of this disease is puking and vomiting. Though there could be other reasons for the vomiting, you should not rule out ECE. The pet might discharge clear mucus at this time.

- The pet will soon get a severe case of diarrhea. You can expect a green colored stool during this time. The mucus causes this color discharge in the pet. Needless to say, the feces will smell really bad.
-
- If the condition of the Pacman frog worsens, he will show symptoms of black feces. The pet might grind his teeth from time to time and you will also notice red colored spots in his mouth. These symptoms mean that Pacman frog is dehydrated and his condition is really bad. He might have developed ulcers. Take him to the vet for treatment without delay.

Treatment:

Try to hydrate the Pacman frog as much as possible. This will help him to feel better. You should look out for the symptoms in your Pacman frog, and if the vomiting and diarrhea episodes seem to increase with time, then you definitely need to see the veterinarian.

The vet will be able to guide you better in terms of medication for the pet. As stated earlier, there could be many other reasons for the prolonged vomiting and diarrhea.

The vet will be a better judge of the symptoms and the condition of the pet. It might pay to keep the pet under his/her observation.

In the initial phase of an infection, the pet will feel nausea and will be restless. He might lose interest in eating and drinking water, but it is more than important that the pet is well fed at this time. You will have to pamper him and make him eat and drink on time.

The vet might prescribe a special diet that will have to be followed. A point that needs to be noted here is that dehydration can often result in mouth ulcers. So, to avoid worsening the condition of the pet, you should take care of his food and water.

No matter how much the pet resists, you have to make sure that he is being well fed when he is recuperating. If the Pacman frog is dehydrated, you can give him Pedialyte with water. In severe cases, you can also give them Gatorade and water, but remember to dilute Gatorade with larger quantities of water.

The veterinarian will suggest the exact dosage of the mixes, which should be 15-20 milliliters of the mix in every four hours. If the pet Pacman frog does not drink the mix on his own, you will have to syringe feed the animal. Be careful while doing this so that the Pacman frog does not develop any infection.

You should also make sure that the pet is eating a nutritious diet to allow his body to heal quickly. You can feed him Gerber chicken baby food, which is highly nutritious and light on the intestine.

It is important that the food is easy on his digestive system. You can also feed the pet with Pacman frogvite along with the baby food. You will notice that the pet will get better with proper food and medication.

As the diarrhea gets better, you might notice that the stool turns from the liquid to a grainy texture. This indicates that the pet is not getting adequate nutrients.

Talk to the vet and work out a diet plan for him where he gets adequate proteins. An important thing that you should know about ECE is that even after your pet has recovered, he is still not free from the virus.

The pet himself will be safe from the condition after acquiring it once. It is known that the virus stays in the Pacman frog's system for over six months. This is a reason that a new Pacman frog is not encouraged to go near the older one for a very long time.

The new one could be carrying the virus, which he could easily transmit to your older Pacman frog.

Gastrointestinal blockage

Gastrointestinal blockage is a very common problem in Pacman frogs. It is even said that it is one of the main causes behind premature death in Pacman frogs. This condition occurs when the Pacman frog has a swollen intestinal tissue.

A Pacman frog might accidentally swallow something dangerous for him, such as a foam or rubber. This will cause the blockage of the digestive tract in the Pacman frog.

The best way to avoid such incidents is to always keep an eye on the pet. The Pacman frog is a curious animal. He will always be running into some kind of trouble if you don't keep an eye on him.

You should make sure that all dangerous items, such as rubber items and foam items, are not in the reach of the pet. Keeping dangerous things out of the sight of the pet is probably the best way to avert all the tension that arises following a gastrointestinal blockage. Such a blockage ruptures the intestine tissue, making digestion of food very difficult for the pet.

Symptoms:

You can look out for the following symptoms in the Pacman frog to know that he is suffering from this particular disease:

- The pet will lose his appetite. You will find him avoiding even his favorite foods. He will not drink water, which could further lead to dehydration.
-
- You will notice a sudden and drastic weight loss in the pet.
-
- Another symptom of this disorder is vomiting.
-
- The pet would be seen struggling during his bowel movements. You should watch out for this symptom.
-
- You will notice the Pacman frog to be very lazy and lethargic.
-
- The pet will suffer from diarrhea.

Treatment:

If you find any of the above symptoms in a Pacman frog, it is important that you waste no time and take the pet to the veterinarian. The vet will conduct X-rays and ultrasounds to confirm the blockage. Don't make the mistake of treating the pet at home.

Usually the symptoms start with vomiting. Severe dehydration follows the bouts of vomiting. If there is a blockage, the Pacman frog would need as surgery. It is important that you are mentally prepared for this.

Lymphoma

Your Pacman frog is also at risk of another disease called Lymphosarcoma. This disease is also called Lymphoma. It occurs because of the uncontrolled growth of the cells in the Pacman frog's body.

Though this is very common in these animals, it can be difficult to detect, especially in the earlier stages.

Pacman frogs of age four and above are at the risk of Lymphoma. Yet, it is also known that a type of Lymphoma can also attack younger Pacman frogs.

You should never take any symptom lightly and should visit the vet when you observe changes in a Pacman frog.

The vet will conduct tests on the blood sample of the pet to confirm this health condition.

Symptoms:

You can look out for the following symptoms in the Pacman frog to know that he is suffering from this particular disease:

- You will notice a sudden and drastic weight loss in the pet.
-
- You will notice the Pacman frog to be very lazy and lethargic. It will appear that he has no energy to do anything.
-
- The pet will suffer from diarrhea.

- The lymph nodes of the pet will also be swollen.
-
- Another symptom that could accompany this disease is a cough. The pet will experience some difficulty in his breathing and will acquire a bad cough.

Treatment:

The treatment that is available for Lymphoma is chemotherapy. This in no way means that the pet will be disease free. The disease can reoccur in about seven to ten months.

It is very difficult to save the pet after he has been diagnosed with this disease. Mostly, it gets detected in later stages, so the treatment becomes all the more difficult.

Because the symptoms of this disease are very general, it is suggested that you ask your veterinarian to conduct yearly tests for your pet.

This would help in detecting any issue in the very beginning, which makes it possible to treat it successfully.

2. Taking care of a sick pet Pacman frog

If your Pacman frog is sick, it is very important that you take him to a qualified veterinarian. It is never advised to self-medicate. For example, if your Pacman frog is suffering from a fever and you decide to give the animal a medicine that you take for fever, then you are in for a shock.

The medicines that work on human beings or other animals might not necessarily work on your Pacman frog. You should never take this chance. Always consult the veterinarian before administering any medicine to the pet.

Along with the medication, you should pamper the sick Pacman frog. Pacman frogs love to be loved and pampered. You will see them recovering fast when you give them your attention and care.

While it will be a little difficult for you to take care of the Pacman frog when he is sick, the experience can actually strengthen the bond that you share with the pet Pacman frog.

The first sign that something is not right with the Pacman frog is the body temperature of the animal. He should ideally be around 102 degrees Celsius. You should check this.

If you feel that the Pacman frog is very warm to touch, then you should know that the pet is not well.

Other symptoms that can help you to know that the pet is unwell include a lazy and lethargic pet. If you feel that the pet is not himself and has been acting very lazily, then this could be because he is unwell.

The pads of the feet of the Pacman frog will also get warm in such a condition. This is another symptom that you should look out for.

When you see the symptoms of a high fever in the pet, the first thing that you should do is make sure that the pet is drinking water. He can be given Pedialyte to help him recover. You should consult a veterinarian if the temperature does not come down in a few hours.

It is very important that you don't ignore the health condition of the Pacman frog. Even if he has a slight fever, you should take it seriously because before you know the slight fever to take shape of a life threatening disease. So, never hesitate to consult a vet in case of any doubts.

After you have consulted the veterinarian, you will have to spend a lot of time with your pet while he is recovering from his illness. This can get very daunting for a new owner because he would not want to commit a mistake while taking care of his beloved pet.

You can take some simple precautions to make sure that your pet is healing better and faster.

To begin with, you should always make sure that the pet is warm and comfortable. The pet will require something to curl into. He will also need his privacy at this time.

If you have more than one Pacman frog, you need to keep the sick pet isolated. This is to give the ill pet time to get better and to avoid spreading the disease.

If there are things and toys that the pets share, you should wash these things nicely and keep them separately. You should wash the bedding and other washable accessories in the cage of the Pacman frog. A pet recovering surgery should be kept in a safe and closed environment so that he does not bruise himself.

A Pacman frog can get dehydrated very easily. The pet might throw up when he is not well. This can easily lead to dehydration. The Pacman frog will get disoriented if he is dehydrated for too long.

You need to make sure that the pet is hydrated at all times. You can pull the skin at the back of the neck of the Pacman frog.

If the skin does not fall back easily, then the pet is definitely dehydrated. The vet might also suggest intravenous injections in severe cases. You should make sure that that the pet does not consume cold water. This can cause severe diarrhea in the pet. Water at room temperature is the best for the Pacman frog.

If the Pacman frog is extremely dehydrated, you can serve him Pedialyte with water to help him get better. In severe cases, you can also give them Gatorade and water, but Gatorade needs to be diluted with larger quantities of water because of its high sugar content.

These fluids will help the Pacman frog to recover faster. Along with these mixes, your pet Pacman frog should have access to simple water at all times.

The veterinarian will suggest the exact dosage of the mixes that your Pacman frog needs depending on his condition. But, in general he should have 15-20 milliliters of the mix in every four hours.

If the pet Pacman frog does not drink the mix on his own, you will have to find a way to make him drink it. You can't force the pet, so the best way to replenish his body during a dehydration phase is to syringe feed him. If you take all the precautionary methods, this is not a difficult method.

To syringe feed the animal, take a clean syringe and fill it with the drink mix. Now, take this syringe to the side of the mouth of the pet. Slowly release a drop at a time in his mouth.

The Pacman frog will not be so easy to feed, so you need to be patient. You need to be careful so that the Pacman frog does not develop any infection.

The pet is not well, so you have to be prepared for extra effort at this time. No matter how much the pet resists, you have to make sure that he is being well fed when he is recuperating. You should also make sure that the pet is taking a nutritious diet to allow his body to heal quickly.

A sick pet will also lose interest in eating his food. You might have to take out time and hand feed him. You can use canned food or baby food that is prescribed by the veterinarian.

It is important that the food is easy on his digestive system. The sick pet needs nutrition, but does not need the pressure of digesting heavy foods.

You can also feed the pet with Pacman frogvite along with the baby food. Pacman frogvite will help the pet to get the much-needed taurine and vitamins in his diet. Make sure that the food is not very hot or cold. It should be warm and just right for the Pacman frog.

Chapter 8: Grooming the Pacman frog

When you decide to keep a Pacman frog as a pet, you should understand that you will have to pay attention to the basic cleaning and grooming of the Pacman frog. This is essential to keep the Pacman frog clean and healthy. Not only will your Pacman frog appear neat and clean, he will also be saved from many unwanted diseases.

When you are looking at grooming sessions for your Pacman frog, you should pay special attention to the Pacman frog's ears, teeth and bathing. This chapter will help you to understand the various dos and don'ts while grooming your pet Pacman frog.

1. Ears

The ears of the Pacman frog need to be cleaned regularly so that there is no wax deposited. There are many owners who might not consider ear cleaning an important part of Pacman frog keeping, but in reality wax can lead to mite infestation and other infections.

In severe cases, the hearing of the pet can be compromised. It is important that you know of the early signs of mite infestation. The wax in the ears will have a light brown color, while the wax with mite will be dark brown in color.

It is important to see the veterinarian in case you have doubts about mite infestation. Don't put any drops in the pet's ears without consulting the vet. In general, you should try to clean the Pacman frog's ears once a week, or at least once in ten days.

You will require a cotton swab and an ear cleaning solution that is used for either Pacman frogs or kittens. If there is somebody in the house who could help you, it will be easier to clean the ears.

If you are the only one doing this task, you should be calm and patient because Pacman frogs don't like their ears being touched and cleaned. You can warm the cleaning solution before use.

Sit comfortably on the floor and hold the Pacman frog gently by the loose skin behind the neck. Use your lap to give support to the Pacman frog's legs. Take a cotton swab and apply some cleaning agent to it.

You should use the cotton swab with the cleaning agent to clean the parts of the ear that are easily visible to you. Don't go too deep because this can hurt the Pacman frog. You should definitely not try to go further in the ear canal.

Repeat the process on both the ears. If you commit a small mistake from your side, it could cost the Pacman frog his hearing. So, you need to make sure that whatever you do is gentle, yet firm hands.

The Pacman frog might get uneasy and might try to get away from your grip. To make sure that the Pacman frog is stable and not jerking, you can give him a treat. This will keep him occupied and will make your job easier.

2. Teeth

When you are considering the overall hygiene and cleanliness of the Pacman frog, you also have to take care of his teeth. You might have problems cleaning the pet Pacman frog's teeth in the beginning, but he will get used it very soon.

As a rule, you should try to clean the teeth once or twice a month. If you ignore his teeth, you will only invite unwanted problems for the Pacman frog. You will notice tar depositing on the teeth if they are not clean. This will automatically lead to tooth decay.

You should also know that many kidney issues in the Pacman frog are also related to its bad oral health. So, it is better to be regular with teeth cleaning procedure of the Pacman frog.

It is also important that you take the pet to the vet if you see any tar on the teeth. Even if all seems fine, it is advised to schedule dental check-ups for the Pacman frog once or twice a year.

You can use toothpaste that is used for kittens and cats. You might also find toothpaste specially designed for the Pacman frogs. Along with the toothpaste, you should use a soft brush that has been specially designed for kittens. A toothbrush with hard bristles might hurt the Pacman frog's jaw, so you should avoid using that.

Your movements should be very soft. If you are too hard, you will hurt the Pacman frog. Be very observant of the lather that comes out from the Pacman frog's mouth. If you see a pink or red color, you should immediately know that it is blood and that you are being too hard on the Pacman frog's mouth.

Many owners complain that the Pacman frog closes its mouth while the teeth are being cleaned. This makes it very difficult for the cleaning to take place. If your Pacman frog does the same, then you can clean only one side of the mouth in one sitting. This means that you will have to be more frequent with the teeth cleaning sessions.

3. Bathing the Pacman frog

Pacman frogs belong to the class of animals that are not extremely fond of bathing. Even within Pacman frogs, there are some that are okay with being in water and there are others that are hydrophobic. You will have to figure out whether your Pacman frog is hydrophobic or not.

If your Pacman frog is scared of water, you will have to try some tricks to get the Pacman frog clean. Even if the Pacman frog is hydrophobic, he needs to take a bath. This is something that you as the owner need to remember. The case of the hydrophobic Pacman frog will be discussed later in this section.

It will be a difficult task for you to bathe your pet, but this is no way means that it is okay for the Pacman frogs to go without bathing. If the pet is not clean, he will attract fleas and other parasites. This only means extra work for you and veterinary visits for the Pacman frog.

To avoid the Pacman frog from getting sick, make sure that the Pacman frog is bathed every now and then. The frequency would depend on the climate and the environment of the Pacman frog. If it is too hot or if the surroundings are not too clean, it means that your pet should be given a bath more often.

Another point that you need to remember here is that while it is important to bathe the Pacman frog once in a while, over-bathing is not recommended. This can also create many problems. The skin of the Pacman frog will begin to lose many important essential oils if they are bathed frequently.

You will be surprised to learn this, but too much bathing can also increase the odor that the Pacman frog might emit. To save yourself from these issues, try to keep things under control. As a rule, give your Pacman frog a bath once in three or four weeks.

When you are looking to give a nice bath to your Pacman frog, you should be looking at two things: a good quality mild shampoo and a few towels. It is very important that you choose the right shampoo for the Pacman frog. If the shampoo is too hard or harsh, it will leave rashes on the Pacman frog and might even cause serious damage to his skin.

You can buy a good quality cat shampoo or a baby shampoo for the Pacman frog. These shampoos are very mild on the skin and have been proven to be ideal for a Pacman frog. You also need a few towels handy for the Pacman frog. While one will be used to dry the water off, the others are required to cover the ground or floor.

If your Pacman frog is suffering from a flea infestation, then you will have to use a shampoo that can help the Pacman frog to get rid of the fleas. You should consult the vet before you use a specialized flea shampoo. It is important not to take a chance on the health of the Pacman frog.

If your Pacman frog is not scared of water it will relatively easier for you to bathe it. But, even if it is there are a few precautions that you need to take. You should understand that how your Pacman frog behaves under water will depend on its individual personality.

It is important that you make a few attempts to understand your pet's personality. Don't give up and understand his behavior and mannerisms. This will only help you in your future dealings with the pet.

To begin with, make sure that the water you are using to bathe the pet is warm. Pacman frogs have a body temperature that is different from human beings. They should be bathed in warm water to keep them safe.

Take a tub and fill it half with warm water. Lift your Pacman frog delicately in your hands. Make sure that your grip is firm. The Pacman frog might surprise you when it touches water and might try to jump out of your hands. To avoid such a situation, place your hands on the stomach area and hold him firmly.

Place the Pacman frog in the tub of warm water for a few seconds. Observe how he responds to water. If you see him enjoying, then your work becomes easier. You can also sprinkle water over the Pacman frog, but if the pet Pacman frog is not enjoying then you need to be quick.

Take him out of the water, and put some shampoo on his back. You should form a good lather with your hands from the ears towards the tail region. Make sure that the pet does not escape when you are shampooing it. You need to have a firm grip on him.

You can also make use of the kitchen sink to give the Pacman frog a bath. The sink will be deep and it will get difficult for the Pacman frog to run away. If the Pacman frog is hydrophobic, it is advised to use to two sinks or tubs. Fill both with water and use them alternately. Keep talking to your pet and make him feel that everything is fine.

You can also give him a treat at this point to divert his attention. Pacman frogs that are scared of water will give you a tough time. You have to be calm and quick. Keep the Pacman frog in water only for a few seconds and keep alternating the tubs to divert the Pacman frog and confuse him a bit.

Another way to bathe your naughty hydrophobic Pacman frog is to sway him under running warm water. Turn the tap on and make sure the water is warm. It should not be cold or too hot. Once you are convinced that the temperature of the water is right for the pet, hold the pet and bring him under the water for a few seconds.

Before he starts to get fidgety, take him away from the water. Now apply some shampoo over the Pacman frog. Keep swaying him under the water until all the shampoo is washed off. It is very important that all the shampoo is washed off; otherwise the Pacman frog's skin will get affected and will show signs of rashes and abrasions.

While you are bathing the Pacman frog, it is important that you protect his face. Water should not enter his eyes or ears. These are sensitive areas and water could cause some damage to them.

Keep him on the towels and use another towel to pat him dry. Make sure that he is absolutely dry before you let him go, otherwise he will stick dust and dirt on his skin.

After the bath is done, place the Pacman frog on a big towel. You should place a few blankets or towels on the floor to keep it warm and tight for the Pacman frog. The Pacman frog will show too much energy at this time. He will try to escape you. You should be very gentle with the pet, otherwise you could harm him.

Chapter 9: Training the Pacman frog

It is very important to train the animal to make him more suitable to a household. By nature, Pacman frogs can be a little ferocious. You will have to train them to tame them.

Like training most other animals, Pacman frog training will also require you to be patient. You will have to do a few trial and errors before you can be sure that your Pacman frog is well trained. You should remember to have fun even during the training phase.

The training phase can be a great opportunity for you to learn more about your little pet. No matter how much you read about a Pacman frog, your pet will have some individual properties that will separate him from the rest of the lot. This is a good time to learn about all these properties.

The more you learn about your pet, the stronger bond you form with him. You should remember to not take the training phase as a cumbersome thing. In fact, take it as an opportunity to form an everlasting bond with your pet. Your pet will also understand you better during this time.

While you have to be regular and stern during this phase, you should not be harsh and rude. Don't beat the Pacman frog and terrorize it. You will only scare the pet and jeopardize your relationship with him. If you have your doubts, it is better to read more about them and then take your decisions regarding the Pacman frog's training phase.

When you are looking at training the Pacman frog, you should be aiming for nip training and litter training above everything else. These trainings are important to help the Pacman frog adjust into the household and also to make things easier you and your family.

1. Nip training of the Pacman frog

When you buy a new Pacman frog, you might notice that the animal has a tendency to nip. This can be uncomfortable and worrisome for you as the owner, but you should know that this is absolutely normal for a Pacman frog and that you can slowly train the Pacman frog not to exhibit such behavior.

The first thing that you should remember is that you should not harm the pet when he nips. This could scare him and will make things worse for you. If you mishandle the pet and try to beat him, he might also try to bite you and harm you. Avoid going down this road and aim at training the Pacman frog well.

It is important that you understand the reason behind a Pacman frog's nipping. More often than not, Pacman frogs do so when they are in a playful mood. If your Pacman frog wants you to play with him, he could just signal you to do so by nipping. Such behavior is quite common in younger Pacman frogs, so don't be surprised when the young Pacman frog nips really hard.

Another reason behind a Pacman frog's nipping is that the animal could be scared. When you bring the pet to your home for the first time, everything around him will be new. It is quite natural for the pet to get scared. This is the reason that nipping is very common in a new pet Pacman frog.

When you know what you can expect from a new pet, it gets easier. Try to understand that he is still uncomfortable in the new surroundings and will require some time to get used to all that is new around him. Give him that space, time and also your understanding.

Nipping comes very naturally to Pacman frogs. In their natural environment, Pacman frogs are known to nip each other, but this does not harm them because of the quality of their skin. If you notice the skin of your pet, you will find it to very thick. This thick skin is a cushion for the Pacman frog.

The thick and tough skin of a Pacman frog will protect against any nipping, but a human being does not have such a tough skin. The Pacman frog might be happy and playful, but his nipping will hurt you, so it is important to train him against such kind of behavior.

As explained earlier, a Pacman frog can exhibit such behavior when they are scared. It should be noted that if the Pacman frog has had a history of abuse, you can expect him to nip more in fear than in a playful mood.

If the pet is very young, he needs to be taught the behavior that is expected of him. He needs to learn to be sociable. He needs to learn that it is not okay to bite people. There are some tips and tricks that will help you to teach him all this.

Every time the pet tries to bite you, you should loudly say the word 'no'. Do it each time, until the Pacman frog starts relating the word 'no' to something that he can't do. Don't beat him because this will only scare him. Just be stern with your words and also actions.

If think that the above trick is not very useful, then you can put the pet in his cage for some time. The pet will eventually understand that this behavior will send him into the cage. The word 'no' and the act of putting into the cage will make the pet more cautious of his behavior.

It should be noted that it will take some time for the Pacman frog to understand this. Until then, just be patient and keep repeating these actions each time he tries to nip you. The Pacman frog will call back on his memory eventually and relate the cage to something punishable.

Another trick to help the Pacman frog understand that he can't nip and bite is to hold him and drag him away from you. Pacman frogs are used to dragging and pulling amongst themselves. They fight, nip and drag each other. The dominant one obviously wins. You need to establish the fact that you are the dominant one in the house.

When you are pulling the Pacman frog away, you need to be very careful. You want to train the pet and not harm him. Use your thumb and the index finger to hold the skin at the back of the Pacman frog's neck. This skin is loose and you will be able to hold it easily.

Look for the reactions of the Pacman frog. He should not be in pain. The idea is to teach him to give up nipping and biting. When you hold him at the back of his neck, gently push him away from you. You might have to repeat this action several times before the Pacman frog understands what is expected of him.

The Pacman frog might also try to give you a good fight when you pull him away. Don't worry because this is something normal and quite natural of the Pacman frog. Pacman frogs play and fight amongst themselves in their natural environment, so he might just try to defend himself and play with you.

There is another trick that can definitely help your training sessions with the Pacman frog. You can apply something bitter on your toes and fingers, so that when the Pacman frog nips you, he gets that bitter taste. When he gets to taste something bitter and terrible on you, he will eventually give up on nipping you.

It is important that the food item that you use is bitter but is not harmful for the Pacman frog. You should know that there are some specially designed bitter foods for Pacman frogs. These food items are prepared keeping in mind the training of the pet Pacman frogs. You can buy various bitter products, such as bitter apple and bitter lemon.

These products are extremely safe for the Pacman frog, so you can use them without any doubts. They render the bitter taste that will disgust the Pacman frog. You just need to apply them or spray them to your toes and tips of the fingers. While you are working hard to train your pet Pacman frog, you should remember that you don't want to do anything that is not right for the pet in the long run.

For example, if you use too much of these bitter food products, the digestive system of the Pacman frog can get upset. You just need to spray a little. This will be enough to get the job done and also not affect the Pacman frog in a negative way. He just needs a little to get the bitter taste in his mouth.

After your pet has tasted the bitter product and is disgusted, you need to make it up to him. Wash off your hands and toes nicely and give the pet a treat. This is important so that the pet is not scared of you and your hands. This will also make him realize that nipping is not accepted, but eating from your hands is.

There are many treats that the Pacman frog can lick. You can find these treats online. You can also treat your pet to these foods, so that he can affectionately lick from your hands. You should remember that the Pacman frog will start ignoring and avoiding you if he only gets to taste bitter stuff from you. Be a teacher to the pet, but remember to be a friendly teacher.

Another point that you need to know while training your pet is that you need to monitor your actions too. You need to figure out whether nipping is a habit with the pet or if he has suddenly started. If the pet has recently started nipping, then it could be something related to you.

It could be the smell of the new lotion or perfume that you started using. Pacman frogs can get attracted to certain kinds of fragrances and this can lead to nipping. You will have to figure out these things to train your pet well.

If the Pacman frog loves a certain lotion that you wear, he will try to lick you and nip you just to get the flavor of that lotion. You can stop wearing the lotion to avoid such incidents. You also need to track what kinds of fragrances attract your pet more. This understanding will help you to train your pet well. You will know what can trigger your pet into nipping and biting.

For the feet, a simple solution is to keep the feet clean and also wearing socks in the house. When you wear socks, the Pacman frog gets a little distracted. There are many owners of Pacman frogs that have reported that wearing socks lead to a reduction of biting and nipping in the Pacman frogs.

Another reason that could be behind your Pacman frog's nipping and biting is that the Pacman frog could be sick. You have to know your pet well to bee able to detect sudden changes in his behavior. If you see the pet being aggressive when you try to play with him, he could be sick.

You should thoroughly examine your pet for any injuries. If you spot an injury, you should take him to the vet. If he looks sick and tired, even then it is a good idea to take him to the vet. You should never postpone such things because this will drastically affect the pet's health.

While you are training your pet, you should remember that the Pacman frog needs to feel comfortable and secure in your presence. You should spend quality time with him. Don't put him in his cage unnecessarily If he is left in the cage unattended all the time, he will become very aggressive. This will encourage his nipping and biting behavior. Always remember that they can bite when they are scared and disappointed.

You should never neglect your pet. The Pacman frog will learn slowly, but you have to be compassionate and kind towards the pet. Treat him when he exhibits good behavior. This will encourage him further.

2. Litter training

A mother Pacman frog will train the young kits to litter in one corner when they litter, but kits are weaned from their mothers very early. The mother does not get a chance to train the kits.

As the owner, you are also the caretaker and the parent for the pet. You will have to teach him stuff that he needs to know when living in a family. Don't get upset when you see your Pacman frog littering everywhere. You can train him to not do so.

To begin with, you should buy a few litter boxes. Keep these boxes in various areas of the house where the Pacman frog is most likely to litter. You should cover the various corners where you have found the litter earlier. In addition, install one box in the cage. Eventually, you want the Pacman frog to litter in the cage itself.

It is believed that a Pacman frog will generally litter in the first fifteen or twenty minutes of waking up. So, there is a chance that the Pacman frog has already littered in the box in the cage. When you open the cage to take him out, check the box and wait until he has used the box.

You should signal the Pacman frog by pointing towards the litter box. The pet should slowly realize that he needs to use the box if he wants to get out of the cage. You should wait near the cage until he is all done.

Another point that you need to understand here is that Pacman frogs are very smart. When the Pacman frog understands that you will let him out of the cage once he uses the litter box, he might pretend to use it. You need to check the box and make sure that he has actually used it.

If you notice that the pet is not using the litter box installed in his cage, then you need to understand why. There is a chance that the litter box is uncomfortable for him. In such a case, you should look to buy a box with a front ledge that is low. This is good for your Pacman frog.

You can even make one for your Pacman frog. If you buy a cat litter box, you will notice that the front ledge is not too low. You could cut in in half to make it suitable for your Pacman frog. The idea is to make it really comfortable for your pet Pacman frog. A suitable litter box will have a back ledge that is high. This gives the right support to the pet.

The Pacman frog will take its own time to adjust to the environment. It is always difficult for a new pet to adjust. If you get him a new cage or if you make any changes in his surroundings, he will find it difficult to adjust, but this problem is only time related and will get solved.

Every time the Pacman frog litters outside the box, place his litter in the box that he should be using. You need to show the pet that he should be using the litter box. This could be difficult for you in the beginning, but the Pacman frog will learn soon. You should place food and toys in areas and corners that you want to save.

When the Pacman frog sees a toy or a food item in a corner, he will try to look for another corner to pass his stools. You can also place a mat underneath the litter box to save your carpet or home mats. Make sure that the mat that you use is waterproof.

Observe your Pacman frog's mannerisms when he is using the litter box. If he has a tendency to bite the mat underneath or stuff kept around, you should discourage this behavior. To do so, you can use the bitter food sprays on the mats and other stuff. This will automatically discourage the pet from biting around when he is littering.

The litter box should definitely be kept clean to maintain the overall hygiene and to prevent diseases. You should wash the box once a week. However, a point that needs to be noted here is that the box should not be too clean. A clean litter box that almost appears new could be appealing to you, but it is a turn off for the Pacman frog.

The Pacman frog will use its sense of smell to use the areas that he has used before. You should leave some paper litter in the box to encourage the pet to use the box again. This is a simple trick that you can use when you are trying to litter train your pet.

When you are buying a litter box, you should remember that the size of the box will depend on the size of your Pacman frog. For example, a male pet Pacman frog will need a bigger box due to his size as compared to the box that a female pet Pacman frog will need.

If you are domesticating more than one Pacman frog in your home, then this will also affect the littering process of the Pacman frogs. This may come as a surprise to you, but the dominant pet could affect how the other pets use the litter boxes in the house.

You might notice that the habits of a dominant pet Pacman frog are influencing the other pet Pacman frogs. The dominant one will always try to boss them around and make the others feel inferior.

Pacman frogs don't like to use the same litter box. The Pacman frogs could also be competing for a litter box. These are the issues that you will have to find out. Observe which Pacman frog is using which litter box and which one suddenly leaves a litter box.

You should make sure that each Pacman frog has his own box, so that he is not left to use the carpets and the floors. Even after you have trained your Pacman frog to use the litter box, you have to be vigilant.

If you are observant, you might face issues. There could be instances when your pet Pacman frog would suddenly give up the use of the litter box. Instead of getting angry on him, it is important that you probe into the reason for his sudden change in behavior.

When the Pacman frog is sick, he might give up the use of the litter box. The main reason behind this is that the pet might not have the strength in his hind legs to get on to the box. He could be suffering from a gastro intestinal or adrenal disease, which could make him weak and lethargic.

You should be cautious when you observe such changes in your pet Pacman frog. Don't ignore his condition, or don't force him to use the litter box. You should not get angry on the pet because he is littering on the floor. It is not his fault if he is not well.

The best thing to do in such a situation is to take the pet to the vet. This will avoid the condition getting worse. He or she will look for the symptoms of various diseases and will help you to understand what is wrong with the pet.

Conclusion

Thank you again for purchasing this book!

I hope this book was able to help you in understanding the various ways to domesticate and care for Pacman frogs.

Pacman frogs are adorable and lovable animals. These animals have been domesticated for many years. Even though they are loved as pets, they are not very common, and there are still many doubts regarding their domestication methods and techniques. There are many things that the prospective owners don't understand about the animal. They find themselves getting confused as to what should be done and what should be avoided.

A Pacman frog is a small, naughty animal that will keep you busy and entertained by all its unique antics and mischiefs. It is said that each animal is different from the other. Each one will have some traits that are unique to him. It is important to understand the traits that differentiate the Pacman frog from other animals. You also have to be sure that you can provide for the animal. So, it is important to be acquainted with the dos and don'ts of keeping the Pacman frog.

If you wish to raise a Pacman frog as a pet, there are many things that you need to understand before you can domesticate the animal. You need to make sure that you are ready in terms of the right preparation. There are certain unique characteristics of the animal that make him adorable, but these traits can also be very confusing for many people. You can't domesticate the animal with all the confusions in your head.

If you are still contemplating whether you want to domesticate the Pacman frog or not, then it becomes all the more important for you to understand everything regarding the pet very well. You can only make a wise decision when you are acquainted will all these and more. When you are planning to domesticate a Pacman frog as a pet, you should lay special emphasis on learning about its behavior, habitat requirements, diet requirements and common health issues.

The ways and strategies discussed in the book are meant to help you get acquainted with everything that you need to know about Pacman frogs. You will be able to understand the unique antics of the animal. This will help you to decide whether the Pacman frog is suitable to be your pet. The book teaches you simple ways that will help you to understand your pet. This will allow you take care of your pet in a better way. You should be able to appreciate your pet and also care well for the animal with the help of the techniques discussed in this book.

Thank you and good luck!

References

http://www.nationalgeographic.com

www.ehow.co.uk

https://en.wikipedia.org

https://www.lovethatpet.com

http://www.Pacman frog-world.com

https://www.thespruce.com

https://www.bluecross.org.uk

https://pethelpful.com

http://www.seniorlink.co.nz

http://www.drsfostersmith.com

www.bbc.co.uk

https://www.cuteness.com

http://www.arkive.org

https://www.hillsborovet.com

www.training.ntwc.org

www.wildlifehealth.org

http://animaldiversity.org

https://www.yourpetspace.info

http://healthypets.mercola.com

https://www.finecomb.com

http://www.marshallpet.com

https://www.all-about-Pacman frogs.com